SH..........

MW01074781

HENRY THE EIGHTH.

WITH

INTRODUCTORY REMARKS

AND

CRITICAL AND EXPLANATORY NOTES.

Adapted for Scholastic or Private Study, and for those qualifying for University and Government Examinations.

BY THE REV. JOHN HUNTER, M.A.
Formerly
Vice-Principal of the National Society's Training Institution, Battersea.

NEW EDITION.

1872.

INTRODUCTORY REMARKS

<small>ON</small>

SHAKSPEARE'S HENRY THE EIGHTH.

I. OF the thirty-seven dramas commonly regarded as the genuine compositions of our immortal bard, and which (with the exception of Pericles) formed the first collected edition of his plays in 1623, ten are denominated Histories, or Chronicle Plays, presenting many of the most interesting features of that portion of our annals which commenced with the thirteenth century and closed about the middle of the sixteenth;—these are King John, Richard II., Henry IV. in 2 parts, Henry V., Henry VI. in 3 parts, Richard III., and Henry VIII.

II. Some of these historical plays are among the earliest productions of Shakspeare's dramatic pen, having been written when he was about 30 years of age; the last one, being descriptive of events the least remote from his own time, seems to have been deferred till he had entered upon his 50th year.* Malone, however, and others, have assigned the first production of Henry VIII. to the year 1601, about two years before the close of Elizabeth's reign; and they have accounted for the reference which Cranmer, towards the end of the play, makes to the successor of Elizabeth, by supposing that Ben Jonson,

---

* Shakspeare was born in April 1564, and died in April 1616, having just completed his 52nd year.

or some other dramatist, altered the play for a revival representation in the reign of James. It certainly appears probable that this drama has in some of its parts been retouched by another than the original hand; but that the first acting of the piece, as composed by Shakspeare, was in 1613, appears equally probable from evidence preserved in some letters of the period, respecting a new play, called Henry the Eighth or All is True, brought out in June of that year at the Globe Theatre. Sir Henry Wotton, writing to his nephew, on 6th July 1613, says, " The king's players had *a new play* called All is True, representing some principal pieces of the reign of Henry the Eighth, which was set forth with many extraordinary circumstances of pomp and majesty. * * * Now, King Henry making a mask at the Cardinal Wolsey's house, and certain cannons being shot off at his entry, some of the paper or other stuff, wherewith one of them was stopped, did light on the thatch. where being thought at first but an idle smoke, and their eyes being more attentive to the show, it kindled inwardly, and ran round like a train, consuming, in less than an hour, the whole house to the very ground."*

If we are justified by such evidence as this in believing that the first representation of Shakspeare's Henry the Eighth is here referred to, we should, perhaps, claim for the same writer the authorship of the Prologue and Epilogue, which some of the commentators have attributed to Ben Jonson. And then we may feel that the poet probably spoke in harmony with a graver cast of thought which may have come upon him in his 50th year, when he said—

* The Globe and the Blackfriars were the two principal London theatres in Shakspeare's time. The former was a public theatre, the latter a private one; but both belonged to the same company of players, Shakspeare himself being for some time one of the proprietors. The Globe, built about 1596, was an hexagonal building, open in the middle over the yard or pit, where the "groundlings" stood, and thatched over the boxes. It was situated at the Bankside, Southwark, near London Bridge, and took its name from an herculean figure supporting the globe, on which were the Latin words, *Totus mundus agit histrionem*, i. e. All the world acts as the player; or, as Shakspeare has said, "All the world's a stage, and all the men and women merely players."

> " I come no more to make you laugh ; things now
> That bear a weighty and a serious brow,
> Sad, high, and working, full of state and woe,
> Such noble scenes as draw the eye to flow,
> We now present."

III. The historical guides followed by Shakspeare in this play are—The Life of Cardinal Wolsey, by *George Cavendish*, The Chronicle of *Raphael Holinshed*, and The Acts and Monuments of the Church, by *John Fox.*

IV. In these authorities Shakspeare found many details requiring only a very slight alteration of the language to give them a dramatic form. The poet did not feel much at liberty to vary from the acknowledged records of such recent times; and hence many portions of his " chosen truth " appear somewhat prosaic. Several passages, indeed, were they printed in the form of prose, would hardly be observed to be metrical.

By no means few, however, are the instances which this play contains, of a transmutation of the plain statements of the chroniclers into poetry of the most exalted kind,—the transmutation being effected sometimes by condensation, sometimes by enlargement, and not unfrequently by mere touches of gentlest delicacy. Nor are the instances few in which the dramatist has enriched his story by the noblest original emanations of poetic sentiment and language.

V. It may be requisite for many youthful readers to be guarded against an erroneous judgment as to the manner in which historical truth is presented in this drama and in Shakespeare's historical plays generally. He often antedates or postdates events. He frequently represents personages as old when they were really young, or as young when they were really old, or as alive when they were actually dead. Of the deviations from *chronological* truth in the present play, the following may be observed :—

The reversal of the decree for taxing the commons (1525), and the examination of Buckingham's surveyor (1521), are in one scene.

The banqueting scene (1526) precedes that of Bucking-

ham's condemnation (1521); in the latter of which is introduced mention of the king's scruples about his marriage
(1527), and of the arrival of Campeggio (1529).

The scene in which Anne is advanced to the dignity of
Marchioness of Pembroke (1532) precedes that of the legatine
court (1529).

In the same scene in which the birth of Elizabeth (1533)
is announced to the king, he converses with Cranmer about the
charge of heresy (1543).

In the council scene, in which Cranmer is accused (1543),
Henry requests him to be godfather at the approaching baptism
(1533).

Now, these instances show that the poet intentionally violated
the order of time; yet so far from introducing confusion into
history hereby, he has really methodised it in its moral ele-
ments, and made it both intelligible and instructive. Coleridge
gives us a just idea of what a dramatic history should be, when
he says, " it is a collection of events borrowed from history, but
connected together, in respect of cause and time, poetically and
by dramatic fiction ; and thus while the unity from mere suc-
cession may be destroyed, it is supplied by *a unity of a higher
order*, which connects the events by reference to the workers,
gives a reason for them in the motives, and presents men in their
causative character."* It is by this principle of dramatic unity,
—often bringing together and accounting for apparent incon-
sistencies of human conduct, and showing some general tendency or significancy of apparently isolated events,—that
Shakspeare has made his countrymen so truly intelligent in
those portions of English history which he has illustrated. His
eye, while it glanced " from heaven to earth, from earth to
heaven," saw and reverenced the interpositions of Providence
in the affairs of men, and then gave such arrangement to human
actions as should exhibit more distinctly and impressively their
convergence towards a heaven-designed issue. He glanced
also from one part to another of the recorded behaviour of an
individual, and thence, through his wonderful knowledge of

* *See* also Spenser's Letter to Sir W. Raleigh, Introd. to the " Faërie Queen."

·the human heart, was enabled to select such specimens of conduct, and to present them in such order, as might vividly rea-
lise to us the whole nature of the individual. He found in
many instances the chronological order of events presenting a
series of desultory things, but by his master mind they were
soon so transposed as to present harmonious and explanatory
pictures. In short, it is his manner of *setting* the facts of history that has made them reflect so fully and powerfully their
real character and import.

VI. The action of this play is commonly described as com-
mencing shortly after the return of the English court from the
Field of the Cloth of Gold in 1520, and terminating with the
christening of the infant princess Elizabeth in 1533, thus ex-
tending over a period of about thirteen years. It should be
observed, however, that Shakspeare anticipates some important
transactions belonging to the year 1543, whereby he has vir-
tually extended the action of the play to within a very few
years of Henry's death. And let it not be supposed that still
there is presented too small a part of the monarch's conduct for
a just exhibition of his character. The genius of Shakspeare
ever loved the path of historic impartiality; and we shall find
that in his Henry the Eighth he has made such a selection and
arrangement of facts as may well serve for a history—the
moral history—of that prince. Not that Henry himself is the
great hero of the piece :—the most important and interesting
"persons of the drama" are Katharine and Wolsey ; yet the
temper and procedure and fate of Wolsey are developments
arising out of Henry's behaviour ; and the display of Katharine's sublime virtue, of her temperate but firm resistance of
injustice, her magnanimity, her charity, her patience and saintly
resignation, is an impressive commentary on the character of
the monarch who treats her so unworthily.

VII. To comprehend all that essentially constituted the moral
history of this tyrant, it was not necessary that the action of the
play should begin earlier than the eleventh year of his reign.
He came to the throne with an undisputed title, the rival pre-
tensions of Lancaster and York being united in his person.

The feudal baronial power had been exhausted by the wars of the Roses; and in the authority of the church was almost the only influence that might affect the absoluteness of the regal supremacy. Henry, therefore, though by no means a sagacious prince, had the policy to concentrate ecclesiastical power as much as possible in the person of one who humoured all his caprices, flattered his sense of greatness, encouraged his love of gaiety, and was both able and willing to save him the trouble of transacting the affairs of state. In the earlier part of his reign, then, we find him characterised chiefly by that natural passion for pleasure and magnificent display which the immense wealth amassed for him in the preceding reign enabled him to gratify; and the opening of the dramatic history fully indicates the predominance of that passion by a recital of the splendours of the Field of the Cloth of Gold,—but manifests at the same time the tendency of such costly pomp to impoverish the state, and prepares our minds for the first great act of rapacity which revealed the hitherto untempted and therefore undeveloped cruelty of Henry's nature.

In the Duke of Buckingham we see a man of popular virtues and accomplishments, possessed of princely opulence, and retaining a lingering trace of the stamp of feudal aristocracy, a man therefore towards whom the jealousy both of Henry and of Wolsey is attracted. Wolsey is impatient of Buckingham's popularity and splendour; Henry is eager to confiscate and enjoy Buckingham's wealth; and an accusation being easily contrived, the voice of the attainted nobleman is soon heard expressing his consciousness of the power of the individual tyranny that has succeeded the feudal age—"The net has fallen upon me;—It will help me nothing to plead mine innocence; —My life is spanned already!"

In connection with the attainder of Buckingham, so feelingly lamented by Katharine, the poet appropriately makes her also warn the king of the evils of an unjust and oppressive exaction;—Wolsey, to whom Henry trusted for the replenishment of the royal coffers, having been imprudent enough to send out commissions for levying a large subsidy from the commons, whence a great deal of resistance and uproar was reported to have arisen. The king is not yet regardless of the popularity he has acquired by his jovial manners and his love of festive splendour, and immediately reverses the decree of taxation ; while Wolsey, solicitous about his own dignity, takes care to circulate reports that through him the king has been induced to remedy the evil.

Meanwhile there are in preparation a splendid revel for the king's gratification at Wolsey's house, and at the same time, and for the king's gratification also, a melancholy sentence against Buckingham at Westminster Hall. The particular banquet described by Cavendish, and chosen for this occasion by Shakspeare, though it took place some years afterwards, was, as Cavendish tells us, only one of a great many such entertainments resorted to by Henry in the course of a year, and therefore could most warrantably be presented by the poet in immediate precedence of the condemnation and execution of Buckingham, to show the heartless barbarity and voluptuous selfishness of the man who afterwards was found ready to enjoy the festivities of a fresh marriage while the blood of his sacrificed queen had scarcely cooled. At that entertainment the passion for Anne Bullen first appears, and the poet soon follows up the scene by making us listen to the "buzzing of a separation between the king and Katharine."

We can imagine with what celerity the impetuous and arbitrary prince would have effected the separation, but for the necessity of securing the church's sanction, and thus providing for his future offspring being acknowledged as legitimate. Hence the opportunity which the legatine court has given to the dramatist for exhibiting the noble merits of Katharine's eloquent remonstrance, and of introducing, as due impartiality demanded, Henry's declaration of his scruples about the validity of his marriage, and his exculpation of Wolsey in reference to suspicions of the cardinal having suggested those scruples. It is nevertheless manifest that love for Anne Bullen is the great reason of Henry's desire for the divorce, and that hatred of Anne Bullen's Lutheran sentiments is the chief cause why

Wolsey, if he really favoured the divorce, endeavoured to delay it.

We now, however, see the arm withdrawn that was wont to lean kindly on Wolsey's shoulder. The mutability of earthly power is about to receive impressive illustration. The voice which had said—

> " My Wolsey,
> The quiet of my wounded conscience,
> Thou art a cure fit for a king"—

is now heard whispering aside—

> " These cardinals trifle with me ; I abhor
> This dilatory sloth, and tricks of Rome.
> My learn'd and well-beloved servant, Cranmer,
> Prithee, return ! with thy approach, I know,
> My comfort comes along."

Wolsey, nevertheless, in fancied security, endeavours to recommend his service to the afflicted queen, and counsels her to avoid such behaviour as might prejudice her interest with the king ; and nobly has the poet's genius expressed here the varying emotions by which Katharine is actuated, according as her sense of honour, of purity, of injury, or of loneliness in a foreign land, is awakened. But with the fall of Katharine, the fall of Wolsey also is impending. In the next Scene we hear the busy tongues of his adversaries anticipating with delight his downfall. The cardinal himself then enters, and all unsuspicious of the departure of his power, settles with himself what the king shall do in the matter of the divorce :—

> " It shall be to the Duchess of Alençon,
> The French king's sister ; he shall marry her.—
> Anne Bullen ! No ; I'll no Anne Bullens for him :
> The late queen's gentlewoman,—a knight's daughter—
> To be her mistress' mistress ! the queen's queen !
> This candle burns not clear ; 'tis I must snuff it ;
> Then out it goes."

How affecting is this prelude to the entrance of Henry, who, with the schedule in his hand, exclaims—

> " What piles of wealth hath he accumulated
> To his own portion !"

Here again is the rapacious monarch on his prey. The wealth which Wolsey has been permitted to acquire must now serve for the promotion of purposes to which Wolsey cannot be instrumental. Wolsey must remain with the church of Rome Henry has resolved to throw off the papal supremacy. In vain therefore the minister asserts his loyalty. He is possessed of too much wealth for one whose "contrary proceedings in the divorce are all unfolded;" and soon the poet affectingly commends the fallen man to our pity, as one who, having hitherto been lost in an artificial character superinduced upon him by circumstances, has now recovered himself, and sees both his own heart and the world's fortunes in their true light.

At the commencement of the Fourth Act, the poet, after making us aware that Katharine had been removed first to the royal manor at Ampthill, and afterwards to that of Kimbolton, introduces the procession from Westminster Abbey to the Palace on the occasion of Anne Bullen's coronation. He then transfers us to Kimbolton, to behold the last sickness and listen to the last words of the repudiated queen. With this the tragical portions of the drama terminate. "The true conclusion" of the piece, Schlegel says, "is the death of Katharine" which Shakspeare "has placed earlier than was conformable to history." 'But as, properly speaking, there is no division in the history where he breaks off, we must excuse him if he gives us a flattering compliment of the great Elizabeth for a fortunate catastrophe. The piece ends with the general joy at the birth of that princess, and with prophecies of the happiness which she was afterwards to enjoy or to diffuse." It is important, however, to observe that the poet's previous introduction of Cranmer, as accused by the Bishop of Winchester and defended by Henry, was intended to illustrate the great national change that had resulted from the papal opposition to the divorce of Katharine, and to complete the moral portraiture of a prince, whose bad passions urged him for their gratification to "break the bonds of Rome," and to assert the religious independence of his realm.

KING HENRY THE EIGHTH

PERSONS REPRESENTED.

(Appears)

KING HENRY VIII. . . . . . Act I. sc. 2; sc. 4. Act II. sc. 2; sc. 4.
Act III. sc. 2. Act V. sc. 1; sc. 2; sc. 4.

CARDINAL WOLSEY . . . . . Act I. sc. 1; sc. 2; sc. 4. Act II. sc. 2;
sc. 4. Act III. sc. 1; sc. 2.

CARDINAL CAMPEIUS . . . . . Act II. sc. 2; sc. 4. Act III. sc. 1.

CAPUCIUS, *ambassador from the*
Emperor Charles V . . . . Act IV. sc. 2.

CRANMER, *archbishop of Canter-*
bury . . . . Act II. sc. 4. Act V. sc. 1; sc. 2; sc. 4.

DUKE OF NORFOLK . . . . . Act I. sc. 1; sc. 2. Act II. sc. 2. Act III.
sc. 2.

DUKE OF BUCKINGHAM . . . . Act I. sc. 1. Act II. sc. 1.

DUKE OF SUFFOLK . . . . . . Act I. sc. 2. Act II. sc. 2. Act III. sc. 2.
Act V. sc. 1; sc. 2.

EARL OF SURREY . . . . . . Act III. sc. 2. Act V. sc. 2.

LORD CHAMBERLAIN . . . . . Act I. sc. 3; sc. 4. Act II. sc. 2; sc. 3.
Act III. sc. 2. Act V. sc. 2; sc. 3

LORD CHANCELLOR . . . . . . Act V. sc. 2.

GARDINER, *bishop of Winchester* Act II. sc. 2. Act V. sc. 1; sc. 2.

BISHOP OF LINCOLN . . . . . Act II. sc. 4.

LORD ABERGAVENNY . . . . . Act I. sc. 1.

LORD SANDS . . . . Act I. sc. 3; sc. 4. Act II. sc. 1.

SIR HENRY GUILDFORD . . . Act I. sc. 4.

SIR THOMAS LOVELL . . . . . Act I. sc. 2; sc. 3; sc. 4. Act II. sc. 1.
Act III. sc. 2. Act V. sc. 1.

SIR ANTHONY DENNY . . . . Act V. sc. 1.

SIR NICHOLAS VAUX . . . . . Act II. sc. 1.

Secretaries to Wolsey . . . . . Act I. sc. 1.

CROMWELL, *servant to* Wolsey . Act III. sc. 2. Act V. sc. 2.

GRIFFITH, *Gentleman-Usher to*
Queen Katharine . . . . . . Act II. sc. 4. Act IV. sc. 2.

Three Gentlemen . . . . Act II. sc. 1. Act IV. sc. 1.

DOCTOR BUTTS, *physician to the*
King . . . . Act V. sc. 2.

Garter King at Arms . . . . . Act V. sc. 4.

Surveyor *to the* Duke of Buckingham . . . . Act I. sc. 2.

BRANDON . . . . Act I. sc. 1.

A Sergeant at Arms . . . . . Act I. sc. 1.

Door-keeper of the Council Cham-
ber . . . . Act V. sc. 2.

Porter, and his Man . . . . . Act V. sc. 3.

Page to Gardiner . . . . Act V. sc. 1.

A Crier . . . . Act II. sc. 4.

QUEEN KATHARINE, *wife to* King
Henry, *afterwards divorced* . . Act I. sc. 2. Act II. sc. 4. Act III. sc. 1.
Act IV. sc. 2.

ANNE BULLEN, *maid of honour*
to Queen Katharine, *and after-*
wards Queen . . . . Act I. sc. 4. Act II. sc. 3.

An old Lady, *friend to* Anne
Bullen . . . . Act II. sc. 3. Act V. sc. 1.

PATIENCE, *woman to* Queen Katharine . . . . Act IV. sc. 2.

Several Lords and Ladies in the dumb shows; Women attending upon the
Queen; Spirits which appear to her; Scribes, Officers, Guards, and other
Attendants.

SCENE,—CHIEFLY IN LONDON AND WESTMINSTER: ONCE, AT
KIMBOLTON.

PROLOGUE.

I come no more to make you laugh; things now
That bear a weighty and a serious brow,
Sad, high, and working,[1] full of state and woe,
Such noble scenes as draw the eye to flow,
We now present. Those that can pity, here
May, if they think it well, let fall a tear:
The subject will deserve it. Such as give
Their money out of hope they may believe,
May here find truth too. Those that come to see
Only a show or two,[2] and so agree
The play may pass,—if they be still and willing,
I'll undertake may see away their shilling
Richly in two short hours.[3] Only they
That come to hear a merry, wanton play,
A noise of targets, or to see a fellow
In a long motley coat guarded with yellow,[4]
Will be deceived; for, gentle hearers, know,

[1] *Working*] Of stirring interest.

[2] *A show or two*] This refers to the show-scenes of the banquet at York Place, Katharine's vision, and the coronation and christening processions. Coleridge calls this drama ' a sort of historical masque, or show-play.'

[3] *In two short hours*] In Shakspeare's time only one play was performed in the day, and it generally lasted about two hours. The performance commenced at one or two o'clock, afternoon.

[4] *In a long motley coat, &c.*] The coat of many colours was the fool's wear. *Guarded* means bound or protected at the edges, bordered.

To rank our chosen truth[1] with such a show
As fool and fight is,—beside forfeiting[2]
Our own brains, and the opinion that we bring
To make that only true we now intend,[3]—
Will leave us never an understanding friend.[4]
Therefore, for goodness' sake,[5] and, as you are known
The first and happiest hearers[6] of the town,
Be sad, as we would make you: Think ye see
The very persons of our noble story,
As they were living; think you see them great,
And followed with the general throng and sweat
Of thousand friends; then, in a moment, see
How soon this mightiness meets misery!
And if you can be merry then, I'll say
A man may weep upon his wedding day.

[1] *Our chosen truth*]   The original title of this play was 'Henry the Eighth, or All is True.'
[2] *Forfeiting, &c.*]   Making fools of ourselves, and failing to fulfil the expectation we have held out.
[3] *We now intend*]   Which we, &c.
[4] *An understanding friend*]   A friend on terms of good understanding with us.
[5] *For goodness' sake*]   To honour goodness.
[6] *The first and happiest, &c.*]   The choicest and most desirable auditors.

KING HENRY THE EIGHTH.

ACT I.

SCENE I.—London. *An Antechamber in the Palace. (Bridewell.)*

Enter the DUKE OF NORFOLK, *at one door; at the other, the* DUKE OF BUCKINGHAM *and the* LORD ABERGAVENNY.

Buck. Good morrow, and well met. How have you done,
Since last we saw[1] in France?
   Nor.   I thank your grace:
Healthful;[2] and ever since a fresh admirer
Of what I saw there.[3]
   Buck.   An untimely ague
Stayed me a prisoner in my chamber, when
Those suns of glory, those two lights of men,
Met in the vale of Andren.

---

[1] *We saw*] We saw each other. So in *Cymbeline*, i. 2, 'When shall we see again?' Compare *ditto*, i. 5, 'Sir, we have known together in Orleans.'

[2] *Healthful*] This—as an answer to the inquiry 'How have you done?'—may be compared with the language in act iv. 2, where to Katharine's inquiry 'How *does* his highness?' Capucius answers, 'Madam, in good health;' and she then says, 'So may he ever *do*.'

[3] *A fresh admirer of, &c.*] Actuated by undiminished wonder at, &c. To *admire* meant to *wonder at*.

Nor.   'Twixt Guynes and Arde :[1]
I was then present; saw them salute on horseback;
Beheld them, when they lighted, how they clung
In their embracement, as they grew together ;[2]
Which had they, what four throned ones could have
       weighed[3]
Such a compounded one ?
     Buck.   All the whole time
! I was my chamber's prisoner.[4]
     Nor.   Then you lost
The view of earthly glory : Men might say, ·
Till this time pomp was single, but now married
To one above itself. [Each following day
Became the next day's master;[5] till the last
Made former wonders its][6] To-day, the French,

---

[1] *'Twixt Guynes and Arde*] Guynes and Ardres, two towns of Picardy, belonged, respectively, to the English and the French. The valley between them was the scene of the famous 'Field of the Cloth of Gold,' in June, 1520. This festivity lasted a fortnight.

[2] *As, &c.*] As if they constituted one person.

[3] *Weighed*] Matched.

[4] *I was my chamber's prisoner*] Buckingham was really present at the interview between Francis and Henry. The dramatist perhaps feigned the duke's absence in order to make occasion for Norfolk's animated description of the grand display.

[5] *Each following day, &c.*] This was a proverbial thought. So in Wheeler's *Treatise of Commerce* (1601), p. 24, 'One day still being a schoolmaster unto the other, and men by experience, &c., growing daily and from time to time to an exacter course.'

[6] *Made former wonders its*] Presented a full display of the wondrous glories thus accumulated. Instead of *its* Shakspeare usually employed the old neuter possessive *his*, as, for instance, a little farther on, where Buckingham says 'Each office did distinctly his full function.' *Its* does not occur in our English Bible, excepting in Levit. xxv. 5, where, however, the word *its* is an unauthorised change of the original *his*.

All clinquant, all in gold, like heathen gods,
Shone down the English; and, to-morrow, they[1]
Made Britain, India: every man that stood
Showed[2] like a mine. Their dwarfish pages were
As cherubins, all gilt: the madams too,
Not used to toil, did almost sweat to bear
The pride[3] upon them, that their very labour
Was to them as a painting:[4] Now this mask
Was cried incomparable;[5] and the ensuing night
Made it a fool and beggar. The two kings,
Equal in lustre, were now best, now worst,
As presence did present them; him in eye
Still him in praise: and, being present both,
'Twas said they saw but one; and no discerner[6]
Durst wag his tongue in censure.[7] When these suns
(For so they phrase them) by their heralds challenged
The noble spirits to arms, they did perform
Beyond thought's compass; that[8] former fabulous story,
Being now seen possible enough, got credit,—
That Bevis was believed.[9]

   - *Buck.*   O, you go far.[10]

[1] *They*] The English.
[2] *Showed*] Here, as frequently in Shakspeare, a verb intransitive signifying *seemed* or *appeared*.
[3] *The pride*] The grand attire.
[4] *Was to them, &c.*] Gave a rosy hue to their complexions.
[5] *Cried, &c.*] Cried up as matchless.
[6] *No discerner*] No one disposed to judge between the two.
[7] *Censure*] Expression of opinion.
[8] *That*] So that.
[9] *That Bevis*] Sir Bevis of Southampton was a prodigy of strength and valour about the time of the Norman Conquest. His famous exploit of subduing the giant Ascapard, whom he afterwards took into his service, is referred to in 2 *King Henry VI.* ii. 3. *See* Ellis's 'Specimens of Early English Metrical Romances.'
[10] *You go far*] You exaggerate. So in *Cymbeline*, i. 1, 'You speak him far.'

Nor. As I belong to worship, and affect
In honour honesty,[1] the tract[2] of everything
Would by a good discourser lose some life,
Which action's self was tongue to.[3]

Buck.   All was royal;
To the disposing of it nought rebelled;
Order gave each thing view; the office did
Distinctly his full function.[4]   Who did guide?—
I mean, who set the body and the limbs
Of this great sport together?

Nor.   As you guess,
One, certes, that promises no element
In such a business.[5]

Buck.   I pray you, who, my lord?

Nor. All this was ordered by the good discretion
Of the right reverend cardinal of York.

Buck. The devil speed him! no man's pie is freed
From his ambitious finger.   What had he
To do in these fierce vanities?   I wonder
That such a keech[6] can with his very bulk

---

[1] *As I be'ong, &c.*]   As I belong to nobility, and in honour am
inclined to honesty.

[2] *The tract*]   The process.   'Tract of time' was anciently a very
common expression.

[3] *Was tongue to*]   Expressed.

[4] *All was royal, &c.*]   Many of the modern editors consider that
this speech, so far as the word 'function,' must have been intended
for Norfolk.   But we may suppose that Buckingham is trying to account for the wonderful effects referred to by Norfolk.   There was
royalty presiding on each side, all was made subservient to that, and
each office performed distinctly its allotted part.

[5] *As you guess, &c.*]   One who, as you guess, does not seem likely
to have had any part in such a business.

[6] *Keech*]   This refers to Wolsey's portly figure, or to his being
a butcher's son.   A *keech* is a lump of fat.

Take up the rays o' the beneficial sun,
And keep it from the earth.

  Nor.   Surely, sir,
There 's in him stuff that puts him[1] to these ends :
For, being not propped by ancestry, whose grace
Chalks successors[2] their way ; nor called upon[3]
For high feats done to the crown ; neither allied
To eminent assistants ;[4] but spider-like,
Out of his self-drawing web,—O ! gives us note,[5]
The force of his own merit makes his way ;
A gift that heaven gives for him,[6] which buys
A place next to the king.

  Aber.   I cannot tell
What heaven hath given him ; let some graver eye
Pierce into that ; but I can see his pride
Peep through each part of him : Whence has he that ?
If not from hell, the devil is a niggard,[7]
Or has given all before, and he begins
A new hell in himself.

  Buck.   Why, the devil,
Upon this French going-out,[8] took he upon him,
Without the privity o' the king, to appoint
Who should attend on him ?[9] He makes up the file
Of all the gentry ;[10] for the most part such

[1] *Puts him*] Disposes and ordains him.

[2] *Successors*] This and the word *confessor* are often accented on the first syllable by Shakspeare and other early writers.

[3] *Called upon*] Called to office or dignity ; preferred.

[4] *Assistants*] Patrons.

[5] *O, gives us note, &c.*] O, he gives us evidence that, &c.

[6] *For him*] In his favour.

[7] *Is a niggard*] Lets no one have any.

[8] *Going-out*] Excursion.

[9] *On him*] On the king.

[10] *He makes up, &c.*] He draws up the list of those nobles who

To whom as great a charge as little honour [1]
He meant to lay-upon : and his own letter
(The honourable board of council out)
Must fetch him in the papers. [2]

   Aber.   I do know
Kinsmen of mine, three at the least, that have
By this so sickened their estates, that never
They shall abound as formerly. [3]

   Buck.   O, many
Have broke their backs with laying manors on them
For this great journey. What did this vanity,
But minister communication of
A most poor issue ? [4]

   Nor.   Grievingly I think,
The peace between the French and us not values
The cost that did conclude it.

   Buck.   Every man,
After the hideous storm [5] that followed, was

---

are to be the king's attendants on this occasion. So Lennox, in
Macbeth, v., says, 'I have a file of all the gentry.'

   [1] *Such to whom, &c.*] Those to whom he meant to lay-on as
much expense as little honour.

   [2] *His own letter, &c.*] A letter from himself, containing no
reference to the honourable board of council, must cause all returns
to be made to him alóne. For 'the papers' the old text has 'he
papers.'

   [3] *So sickened, &c.*] So impoverished their estates that they will
never become as productive as before. Many of the nobles so bur-
dened their estates with debts contracted for the purchase of costly
apparel, that no subsequent frugality could disencumber them.

   [4] *Minister communication, &c.*] Only yield to each party a share
in the poverty and meanness of the issue.

   [5] *After the hideous storm, &c.*] Holinshed says, 'Monday, 18th
June (1520), was such a hideous storm, that many conjectured it did
prognosticate trouble and hatred to follow between princes.'

A thing inspired ; and, not consulting,[1] broke
Into a general prophecy,—That this tempest,
Dashing the garment of this peace, aboded
The sudden breach on 't.

Nor.   Which is budded out ;[2]
For France hath flawed the league, and hath attached[3]
Our merchants' goods at Bourdeaux.

Aber.   Is it therefore
The ambassador is silenced ?[4]

Nor.   Marry, is 't.

Aber. A proper title of a peace ! and purchased
At a superfluous rate ![5]

Buck.   Why, all this business
Our reverend cardinal carried.[6]

Nor.   Like it your grace,[7]
The state takes notice of the private difference
Betwixt you and the cardinal.   I advise you
(And take it from a heart that wishes towards you
Honour and plenteous safety), that you read
The cardinal's malice and his potency

---

[1] *Not consulting*] No man discussing the subject with another; independently of any communication with another.

[2] *Is budded out*] Is brought forth, or brought to pass.   There is here a playful reference to *aboded*.

[3] *Attached*] Seized.

[4] *Is it therefore, &c.*]   Is it on that account that the French ambassador has been denied audience here?

[5] *A proper title, &c.*]   The silencing of an ambassador (an ambassador made to hold his *peace*) is a goodly title-deed of a peace truly, and purchased at an extravagant rate.

[6] *All this business, &c.*]   Not only the interview, but also the violation of the treaty, was brought about by Wolsey.   *See* what is said, farther on, by Buckingham, about the Emperor Charles bribing Wolsey ' to alter the king's course, and break the peace.'

[7] *Like it your grace*]   May it like or please your grace.

Together : to consider further, that
What his high hatred would effect wants not
A minister in his power :[1] You know his nature,
That he's revengeful ; and I know his sword
Hath a sharp edge : it's long, and 't may be said,
It reaches far ; and where 't will not extend,
Thither he darts it.   Bosom up my counsel ;
You 'll find it wholesome.   Lo, where comes that rock
That I advise your shunning.

Enter CARDINAL WOLSEY (*the purse borne before him*),
certain of the Guard, and two Secretaries *with papers.
The* CARDINAL *in his passage fixeth his eye on* BUCKING-
HAM, *and* BUCKINGHAM *on him, both full of disdain.*

Wol. The duke of Buckingham's surveyor ? ha ?
Where 's his examination ?[2]
1 *Secr.*   Here, so please you.
Wol. Is he in person ready ?
1 *Secr.*   Ay, please your grace.
Wol. Well, we shall then know more ; and Buckingham
Shall lessen this big look.[3]
                [*Exeunt* WOLSEY *and Train.*
Buck. This butcher's cur is venom-mouthed, and I
Have not the power to muzzle him ; therefore, best
Not wake him in his slumber.   A beggar's book
Out-worths a noble's blood.[4]
    Nor.   What, are you chafed ?

---

[1] *A minister, &c.*]   A means of effecting it in the power which he
wields.
[2] *Where 's his examination ?*]   Where is he to be examined ?   The
name of this steward was Charles Knyvett.
[3] *This big look*]   *See* the preceding stage direction.
[4] *A beggar's book, &c.*]   A beggar's learning outweighs a nobleman's rank.

Ask God for temperance; that's the appliance only
Which your disease requires.

 Buck.   I read in his looks
Matter against me; and his eye reviled
Me, as his[1] abject object; at this instant
He bores[2] me with some trick: He's gone to the king;
I 'll follow, and out-stare him.

 Nor.   Stay, my lord,
And let your reason with your choler question
What 't is you go about: To climb steep hills
Requires slow pace at first: Anger is like
A full-hot horse; who being allowed his way,
Self-mettle tires him. Not a man in England
Can advise me like you: be to yourself
As you would to your friend.

 Buck.   I'll to the king,
And from a mouth of honour quite cry down
This Ipswich fellow's insolence; or proclaim
There 's difference in no persons.[3]

 Nor.   Be advised,
Heat not a furnace for your foe so hot
That it do singe yourself:[4] We may outrun,
By violent swiftness, that which we run at,
And lose by over-running. Know you not
The fire that mounts the liquor till it run o'er,
In seeming to augment it, wastes it? Be advised:
I say again, there is no English soul
More stronger to direct you than yourself;

---

[1] *His*] Its.

[2] *Bores*] Is undermining.

[3] *Difference in no persons*] No distinction in birth-right, not even
for royalty itself.

[4] *That it do singe yourself*] An allusion to the book of *Daniel*,
iii. 19, 22.

If with the sap of reason you would quench,
Or but allay, the fire of passion.[1]
  Buck.   Sir,
I am thankful to you; and I 'll go along
By your prescription :—but this top-proud fellow,
(Whom from the flow of gall I name not, but
From sincere motions,[2]) by intelligence,
And proofs as clear as founts in July, when
We see each grain of gravel, I do know
To be corrupt and treasonous.
  Nor.   Say not treasonous.
  Buck. To the king I 'll say 't ; and make my vouch as
            strong
As shore of rock. Attend. This holy fox,
Or wolf, or both (for he is equal ravenous
As he is subtle; and as prone to mischief,
As able to perform it : his mind and place
Infecting one another, yea, reciprocally[3]),
Only to show his pomp as well in France,
As here at home, suggests[4] the king our master
To this last costly treaty, the interview,
That swallowed so much treasure, and like a glass
Did break i' the rinsing.[5]
  Nor.   Faith, and so it did.

[1] *If with the sap, &c.*] Compare *Hamlet,* iii. 4, 'Upon the heat and flame of thy distemper sprinkle cool patience.'

[2] *Whom from the flow, &c.*] Whom I do not call so out of malignity, but from honest emotion or indignation.

[3] *His mind and place, &c.*] His mischievous inclination making his office serve to do mischief, and his office, by giving him power to do mischief, tempting his mind to be mischievous.

[4] *Suggests*] Prompts.

[5] *Did break i' the rinsing*] Broke in the first handling or application ; proved itself unable to keep what was put in it.

Buck. Pray, give me favour, sir. This cunning car-
        dinal
The articles o' the combination[1] drew
As himself pleased; and they were ratified,
As he cried, Thus let be: to as much end,
As give a crutch to the dead: But our count-cardinal[2]
Has done this, and 't is well; for worthy Wolsey,
Who cannot err, he did it. Now this follows
(Which, as I take it, is a kind of puppy
To the old dam, treason),—Charles the emperor,
Under pretence to see the queen his aunt,
(For 't was, indeed, his colour;[3] but he came
To whisper Wolsey), here makes visitation:
His fears were, that the interview betwixt
England and France might, through their amity,
Breed him some prejudice; for from this league
Peeped harms that menaced him: He privily
Deals with our cardinal; and, as I trow,—
Which I do well, for I am sure,—the emperor
Paid ere he promised;[4] whereby his suit was granted
Ere it was asked;—but when the way was made,
And paved with gold, the emperor thus desired,
That he would please to alter the king's course,
And break the foresaid peace. Let the king know,
(As soon he shall by me,) that thus the cardinal
Does buy and sell his honour[5] as he pleases,
And for his own advantage.

[1] *The articles of the combination*] These may be seen in the old
Chronicles.
[2] *Our count-cardinal*] Wolsey, as archbishop of York, was a
Count Palatine.
[3] *Colour*] Pretext, or ostensible purpose.
[4] *Paid ere he promised*] Gave a bribe before Wolsey promised.
[5] *His honour*] The king's honour.

Nor.   I am sorry
To hear this of him ; and could wish he were
Something mistaken in 't.[1]

Buck.   No, not a syllable ;
I do pronounce him in that very shape
He shall appear in proof.

Enter BRANDON ; *a Sergeant at Arms before him, and two*
*   or three of the Guard.*

    Bran. Your office, sergeant : execute it.

    Serg.   Sir,
My lord the duke of Buckingham, and earl
Of Hereford, Stafford, and Northampton, I
Arrest thee of high treason, in the name
Of our most sovereign king.

    Buck.   Lo you,[2] my lord,
The net has fallen upon me : I shall perish
Under device and practice.[3]

    Bran.   I am sorry
To see you ta'en from liberty to look on
The business present :[4] 'Tis his highness' pleasure,
You shall to the Tower.

    Buck.   It will help me nothing
To plead my innocence ; for that die[5] is on me,
Which makes my whitest part black. The will of heaven
Be done in this and all things !—I obey.—
O my lord Aberga'ny, fare you well.

    [1] *Something mistaken*] Misjudged in some part of what you say.
Norfolk speaks rather favourably of Wolsey throughout this scene ;
but far otherwise after the arrest of Buckingham.

    [2] *Lo you*] Look you ; see.

    [3] *Practice*] Contrivance.

    [4] *To look on, &c.*] To attend to such a business as this.

    [5] *That die*] There is here a quibble between the *dye* or stain of
attainder, and the cast of the *die* in hazard.

Bran. Nay, he must bear you company:—The king
                                    [*To* ABERGAVENNY.
Is pleased you shall to the Tower, till you know
How he determines further.
    Aber.   As the duke said,
The will of heaven be done, and the king's pleasure
By me obeyed.
    Bran.   Here is a warrant from
The king, to attach [1] lord Montacute, and the bodies
Of the duke's confessor, John de la Car,
One Gilbert Peck, his chancellor,—
    Buck.   So, so;
These are the limbs of the plot: no more, I hope.
    Bran. A monk o' the Chartreux.
    Buck.   Nicholas Hopkins?
    Bran.   He.
    Buck. My surveyor is false; the o'ergreat cardinal
Hath showed him gold.   My life is spanned already :
I am the shadow of poor Buckingham,
Whose figure even this instant cloud puts on,
By darkening my clear sun.[2]—My lords, farewell. [*Exeunt.*

---

  [1] *To attach*]. To arrest.
  [2] *I am the shadow, &c.*] I am the shadow of my former self,
which former self stands between me and the bright future I had in
prospect, and turns a dark side towards me.   The difficulty here is
removed by observing that the duke compares his life to the *span of
heaven*, which ended before his sun went down, or while his sun was
yet clear.   Young has a similar comparison in his *Seventh Night*,—
' Men perish in advance, as if the sun should set ere noon.'

SCENE II.—*The Council Chamber.*

Cornets.   *Enter* KING HENRY, CARDINAL WOLSEY, *the* Lords *of the Council,* SIR THOMAS LOVELL, Officers, *and* Attendants.   *The* KING *enters, leaning on the* CARDINAL'S *shoulder.*

K. Hen. My life itself, and the best part of it,
Thanks you for this great care: I stood i' the level [1]
Of a full-charged confederacy; and give thanks
To you that choked it.—Let be called before us
That gentleman of Buckingham's: in person
I 'll hear him his confessions justify; [2]
And, point by point, the treasons of his master
He shall again relate.

The KING *takes his State.*[3]   *The* Lords *of the Council take their several places. The* CARDINAL *places himself under the* KING'S *feet, on his right side.*

A noise within, crying, Room for the Queen !   *Enter the* QUEEN, *ushered by the* DUKES OF NORFOLK *and* SUFFOLK : *she kneels. The* KING *riseth from his State, takes her up, kisses, and places her by him.*

Q. Kath. Nay, we must longer kneel; I am a suitor.
K. Hen. Arise, and take place by us:—Half your suit
Never name to us; you have half our power;
The other moiety, ere you ask, is given;
Repeat your will, and take it.
    Q. Kath.   Thank your majesty.

---

[1] *I' the level*] Exposed to the aim.
[2] *In person, &c.*] I will hear him in his own person confirm what the cardinal says he has confessed.
[3] *State*] A state was the stage name for a canopied throne.

That you would love yourself, and, in that love,
Not unconsidered leave your honour, nor
The dignity of your office, is the point
Of my petition.

   K. Hen.   Lady mine, proceed.

   Q. Kath. I am solicited,[1] not by a few,
And those of true condition,[2] that your subjects
Are in great grievance : there have been commissions [3]
Sent down among them, which have flawed the heart
Of all their loyalties;—wherein, although,
My good lord cardinal, they vent reproaches
Most bitterly on you, as putter-on
Of these exactions, yet the king our master,
(Whose honour heaven shield from soil! [4]) even he escapes not
Language unmannerly, yea, such which breaks
The sides of loyalty, and almost appears
In loud rebellion.

   Nor.   Not almost appears,—
It doth appear : for, upon these taxations,
The clothiers all, not able to maintain
The many to them 'longing, have put off
The spinsters, carders, fullers, weavers, who,
Unfit for other life, compelled by hunger
And lack of other means, in desperate manner,
Daring the event to the teeth, are all in uproar,
And Danger serves among them.[5]

   K. Hen.   Taxation !

   [1] *I am solicited*] My attention is drawn to the circumstance.

   [2] *Of true condition*] Well affected; loyal. *Condition* means *disposition*.

   [3] *Commissions*] Mandates or warrants; instructions to commissioners to levy taxes or benevolences.

   [4] *From soil*] From being sullied.

   [5] *Danger serves among them*] Danger of starvation is their leader, is that which impels them. Holinshed relates that the duke of Nor-

Wherein? and what taxation?—My lord cardinal,
You that are blamed for it alike with us,
Know you of this taxation?

Wol.   Please you, sir,
I know but of a single part, in aught
Pertains to the state;[1] and front but in that file
Where others tell steps with me.[2]

Q. Kath.   No, my lord,
You know no more than others; but you frame
Things that are known alike,[3] which are not wholesome
To those which would not know them, and yet must
Perforce be their acquaintance.[4]   These exactions
Whereof my sovereign would have note,[5] they are
Most pestilent to the hearing; and to bear them,
The back is sacrifice to the load.   They say
They are devised by you; or else you suffer
Too hard an exclamation.[6]

K. Hen   Still *exaction*![7]
The nature of it?   In what kind, let's know,
Is this exaction?

Q. Kath.   I am much too venturous
In tempting of your patience; but am boldened

folk having asked some of the malcontents what was their captain's name? a person named Greene said, 'that *Poverty* was their
captain, the which with his cousin *Necessity* had brought them to
that doing.'

[1] *I know, &c.*]   I know only as one out of many in aught that
pertains, &c.

[2] *And front, &c.*]   And I merely move in one front with the rest
of the council, who march at the same rate as I do.

[3] *Known alike*]   Known by others as well as yourself.

[4] *Be their acquaintance*]   Know them.

[5] *Would have note*]   Would be informed.

[6] *You suffer, &c.*]   You are too severely censured.

[7] *Still exaction*]   You keep on saying *exaction*.

Under your promised pardon. The subject's grief [1]
Comes through commissions, which compel from each
The sixth part of his substance, to be levied
Without delay : and the pretence for this
Is named, your wars in France : This makes bold mouths;
Tongues spit their duties out ; [2] and cold-hearts freeze
Allegiance in them ; their curses now
Live where their prayers did ; and it 's come to pass,
That tractable obedience is a slave [3]
To each incensèd will.   I would your highness
Would give it quick consideration, for
There is no primer business.

    K. Hen.   By my life,
This is against our pleasure.

    Wol.   And for me,
I have no further gone in this, than by
A single voice ; and that not passed me,[4] but
By learned approbation of the judges. If I am
Traduced by ignorant tongues, which neither know
My faculties, nor person,[5] yet will be
The chronicles [6] of my doing,—let me say
'Tis but the fate of place,[7] and the rough brake
That virtue must go through. We must not stint
Our necessary actions, in the fear
To cope malicious censurers ; [8] which ever,

    [1] *Grief*] Grievance.
    [2] *Tongues spit, &c.*] Tongues contemptuously renounce their
duties.
    [3] *Is a slave*] Seems slavery.
    [4] *Passed me*] Passed my lips.
    [5] *My faculties, &c.*] The extent of my official powers, nor my
personal character.
    [6] *Chronicles*] Reporters.
    [7] *Place*] Office.
    [8] *To cope, &c.*] To encounter malicious critics.

As ravenous fishes, do a vessel follow
That is new trimmed; but benefit no further
Than vainly longing.   What we oft do best,
By sick interpreters, once weak ones, is
Not ours, or not allowed; [1] what worst, as oft,
Hitting a grosser quality, is cried up
For our best act.[2]   If we shall stand still,
In fear our motion will be mocked or carped at,
We should take root here where we sit, or sit
State statues only.

   K. Hen.   Things done well,
And with a care, exempt themselves from fear;
Things done without example,[3] in their issue
Are to be feared.   Have you a precedent
Of this commission?   I believe, not any.
We must not rend our subjects from our laws,
And stick them in our will.[4]   Sixth part of each?
A trembling contribution ! [5]   Why, we take
From every tree, lop,[6] bark, and part o' the timber;
And, though we leave it with a root, thus hacked
The air will drink the sap.   To every county
Where this is questioned,[7] send our letters, with
Free pardon to each man that has denied

    [1] *By sick interpreters, &c.*]   Is by ill-disposed or else undiscerning
interpreters either denied to be our doing, or not approved.
    [2] *What worst, &c.*]   And what we do worst, as gratifying some
baser feeling, is as often extolled for our best act.
    [3] *Example*]   Precedent.
    [4] *Stick them, &c.*]   Place them under the dominion of our own
private will.
    [5] *A trembling contribution*]   A contribution which might well
occasion trembling.
    [6] *Lop*]   The lop-wood or branches.
    [7] *Questioned*]   Disputed, resisted.

The force[1] of this commission : Pray look to 't ;
I put it to your care.
    Wol.   A word with you. [*To the* Secretary.
Let there be letters writ to every shire,
Of the king's grace and pardon.   The grieved commons
Hardly conceive of me ; [2] let it be noised,
That through our intercession this revokement
And pardon comes : I shall anon advise you
Further in the proceeding.   [*Exit* Secretary.

Enter Surveyor.

    Q. Kath. I am sorry that the duke of Buckingham
Is run in [3] your displeasure.
    K. Hen.   It grieves many :
The gentleman is learn'd, and a most rare speaker ;
To nature none more bound ; [4] his training such
That he may furnish and instruct great teachers,
And never seek for aid out of himself.   Yet see,
When these so noble benefits shall prove
Not well disposed,[5] the mind growing once corrupt,
They turn to vicious forms, ten times more ugly
Than ever they were fair.   This man so complete,[6]
Who was enrolled 'mongst wonders, and when we
Almost, with ravished listening, could not find
His hour of speech a minute,—he, my lady,
Hath into monstrous habits put the graces

   [1] *The force*]   The authority.
   [2] *The grieved commons, &c.*]   The aggrieved people have hard
thoughts of me.
   [3] *Is run in*]   Has incurred.   Katharine's interference in behalf
of Buckingham is in fine accordance with her character, but is not
matter of history.
   [4] *Bound*]   Indebted.
   [5] *Disposed*]   Regulated.
   [6] *Complete*]   Accomplished.

That once were his, and is become as black
As if besmeared in hell. Sit by us; you shall hear
(This was his gentleman in trust)[1] of him
Things to strike honour sad.—Bid him recount
The fore-recited practices; whereof
We cannot feel too little, hear too much.

Wol. Stand forth: and with bold spirit relate what you,
Most like[2] a careful subject, have collected
Out of the duke of Buckingham.

K. Hen.   Speak freely.

Surv. First, it was usual with him, every day
It would infect his speech, That if the king
Should without issue die, he 'd carry it so[3]
To make the sceptre his: These very words
I have heard him utter to his son-in-law,
Lord Aberga'ny; to whom by oath he menaced
Revenge upon the cardinal.

Wol.   Please your highness, note
His dangerous conception in this point.
Not friended by his wish,[4] to your high person
His will is most malignant; and it stretches
Beyond you, to your friends.

Q. Kath.   My learn'd lord cardinal,
Deliver all with charity.

K. Hen.   Speak on:
How grounded he his title to the crown,

[1] *His gentleman in trust*] His steward or surveyor. The sentence
would read better if the words 'of him' preceded the parenthetic
clause.

[2] *Most like*] Thoroughly or truly like.

[3] *Carry it so*] Manage matters so as.

[4] *Not friended, &c.*] Not being gratified in his desire of your
dying childless.

Upon our fail?[1] to this point hast thou heard him
At any time speak aught?
   Surv.   He was brought to this
By a vain prophecy of Nicholas Henton.[2]
   K. Hen. What was that Henton?
   Surv.   Sir, a Chartreux friar,
His confessor; who fed him every minute
With words of sovereignty.
   K. Hen.   How knowest thou this?
   Surv. Not long before your highness sped to France,
The duke, being at the Rose,[3] within the parish
Saint Lawrence Poultney, did of me demand
What was the speech among the Londoners
Concerning the French journey: I replied,
Men feared the French would prove perfidious,
To the king's danger. Presently the duke
Said, 'T was the fear, indeed; and that he doubted,[4]
'T would prove the verity of certain words
Spoke by a holy monk: 'that oft,' says he
'Hath sent to me, wishing me to permit
John de la Car, my chaplain, a choice hour
To hear from him a matter of some moment:
Whom after, under the confession's seal,
He solemnly had sworn,[5] that, what he spoke,
My chaplain to no creature living, but

[1] *Fail*] Fail of issue to succeed us.
[2] *Nicholas Henton*] Nicholas Hopkins of the convent of Henton, near Bristol.
[3] *The Rose*] This was the name of a portion of Southwark in which the Duke of Buckingham had a residence, called by the Chroniclers 'The Manor of the Rose in St. Lawrence Pountney.'
[4] *Doubted*] Suspected, surmised.
[5] *Whom after, &c.*] Whom when he had solemnly caused to swear under the seal of confession.

To me, should utter, with demure confidence [1]
This pausingly [2] ensued—Neither the king, nor his heirs,
(Tell you the duke) shall prosper : bid him strive
To gain the love of the commonalty ; the duke
Shall govern England.'
    Q. Kath.   If I know you well,
You were the duke's surveyor, and lost your office
On the complaint o' the tenants : Take good heed
You charge not in your spleen a noble person,
And spoil your nobler soul ! [3]   I say, take heed ;
Yes, heartily beseech you.
    K. Hen.   Let him on :—
Go forward.
    Surv.   On my soul, I 'll speak but truth.
I told my lord the duke, by the devil's illusions
The monk might be deceived ; and that 't was dangerous
    for him
To ruminate on this so far, until
It forged him some design, which, being believed,
It was much like to do : [4] He answered, ' Tush !
It can do me no damage : ' adding further,
That, had the king in his last sickness failed,
The cardinal's and sir Thomas Lovell's heads
Should have gone off.
    K. Hen.   Ha ! what ? so rank ? Ah, ha !
There 's mischief in this man : Canst thou say further ?
    Surv. I can, my liege.
    K. Hen.   Proceed.

---

[1] *With demure confidence*] In a grave confidential manner.
[2] *Pausingly*] With pausing intervals ; slowly and deliberately.
[3] *Your nobler soul*] The nobler dignity of your soul.
[4] *Until it forged, &c.*] Until it might strike out, or form, in his mind some plan for obtaining the crown, which, if he put faith in the *prophecy*, it was very likely to do.

Surv.   Being at Greenwich,
After your highness had reproved the duke
About sir William Blomer,—
    K. Hen.   I remember
Of such a time—Being my sworn servant,[1]
The duke retained him his.——But on ; What hence ?[2]
    Surv. ' If,' quoth he, ' I for this had been committed,
As, to the Tower, I thought,—I would have played
The part my father meant to act upon
The usurper Richard ; who, being at Salisbury,
Made suit to come in his presence ; which if granted,
As he made semblance of his duty, would
Have put his knife into him.'
    K. Hen.   A giant traitor !
    Wol. Now, madam, may his highness live in freedom,
And this man out of prison ?
    Q. Kath.   God mend all !
    K. Hen. There 's something more would out of thee ?
        what say'st ?
    Surv. After —' the   duke   his   father,'—with ' the
        knife—,'
He stretched him, and with one hand on his dagger,
Another spread on his breast, mounting his eyes,
He did discharge a horrible oath ; whose tenour
Was,—were he evil used, he would outgo
His father, by as much as a performance
Does an irresolute purpose.

---

    [1] *Being my sworn servant*] Anciently not only the servants of
the sovereign but also those of the nobles and other persons of distinction took an oath of fidelity at the time of their engagement.
In *Cymbeline*, ii. 4, Posthumus says, ' Her attendants are all sworn
and honourable.'
    [2] *What hence?*] What hence ensued ?

Hen.   There 's his period,[1]
To sheath his knife in us. He is attached:[2]
Call him to present trial: if he may
Find mercy in the law, 't is his; if none,
Let him not seek 't of us: by day and night,[3]
He 's traitor to the height![4]   [*Exeunt.*

SCENE III.—A *Room in the Palace.*

Enter the LORD CHAMBERLAIN *and* LORD SANDS.

Cham. Is 't possible the spells of France should juggle
Men into such strange mysteries?[5]
Sands.   New customs,
Though they be never so ridiculous,
Nay, let them be unmanly, yet are followed.
Cham. As far as I see, all the good our English
Have got by the late voyage, is but merely
A fit or two 'o the face;[6] but they are shrewd ones;
For when they hold them, you would swear directly
Their very noses had been counsellors
To Pepin, or Clotharius,[7] they keep state so.

[1] *There's his period*] There is his purposed consummation.

[2] *Attached*] Arrested.

[3] *By day and night*] In *Hamlet*, i., we find Horatio using the adjuration 'O day and night!'

[4] *Traitor to the height*] Guilty of high treason in the highest degree.

[5] *Juggle men, &c.*] Turn men into such strange curiosities.

[6] *A fit or two o' the face*] A few grimaces.

[7] *Clotharius*] Clothaire and Pepin were early kings of France, the former in 560, the latter in 571. Clotharius is a Latinised form of the name Clothaire, originating from records being in former times so commonly written in Latin. Similarly, in this play, we have Campeius for Campeggio, and Capucius for Chapuys.

Sands. They have all new legs, and lame ones; one
      would take it,
That never saw them pace before, the spavin,
A springhalt, reigned among them.
  Cham.   Death![1] my lord,
Their clothes are after such a pagan cut too,
That, sure, they have worn out christendom.[2]   How now?
What news, sir Thomas Lovell?

Enter SIR THOMAS LOVELL.

  Lov.   Faith, my lord,
I hear of none, but the new proclamation [3]
That 's clapped upon the court-gate.
  Cham.   What is 't for
  Lov. The reformation of our travelled gallants,
That fill the court with quarrels, talk, and tailors.
  Cham. I am glad 't is there; now I would pray our
      monsieurs
To think an English courtier may be wise,
And never see the Louvre.[4]
  Lov.   They must either
(For so run the conditions) leave those remnants
Of fool-and-feather [5] that they got in France,
With all their honourable points of ignorance,

---

[1] *Death!*] *'s death!* was a profane asseveration, an abbreviation
of ' by His death,' as *'s blood* was of ' by His blood,' and *zounds*, that
is, *'s wounds*, of ' by His wounds.'

[2] *They have worn out, &c.*] They have retained nothing of the
costume of Christians.

[3] *The new proclamation*] A sumptuary law for the repression of
extravagance.

[4] *And never see, &c.*] In spite of never having been at the French
court.

[5] *Leave those remnants, &c.*] Leave off those appendages of the
feather-bedecked fool. The fools or jesters wore feathers in their

Pertaining thereunto (as fights, and fireworks; [1]
Abusing better men than they can be,
Out of a foreign wisdom), renouncing clean
The faith they have in tennis and tall stockings,
Short blistered [2] breeches, and those types of travel,[3]
And understand again like honest men;
Or pack to their old playfellows: there, I take it,
They may, *cum privilegio*, wear away
The lag end of their lewdness, and be laughed at.

Sands. 'T is time to give them physic, their diseases
Are grown so catching.

Cham.   What a loss our ladies
Will have of these trim vanities!

Lov.   Ay, marry,
There will be woe indeed.

Sands.   I am glad they 're going;
For, sure, there 's no converting of them; now,
An honest country lord, as I am, beaten
A long time out of play,[4] may bring his plainsong,
And have an hour of hearing; and, by 'r lady,
Held current music too.[5]

Cham.   Well said, lord Sands;
Your colt's tooth is not cast yet.[6]

---

caps. The allusion, however, may be to the feather fans which some
fops were in the habit of carrying.

[1] *As fights and fireworks*] As exhibitions of fighting and fireworks. Steevens says that some very extraordinary fireworks were
played off on the evening of the last day of the royal interview; and
that hence these travelled gallants may have become fond of pyro-
techny.

[2] *Blistered*] Puffed.

[3] *Types of travel*] Signs of foreign experience.

[4] *Beaten, &c.*] Long superseded or excluded by these rivals.

[5] *Held current music*] Have it recognised as good music.

[6] *Your colt's tooth, &c.*] You have not yet laid aside the spirit,

Sands.   No, my lord;
Nor shall not, while I have a stump.
    Cham.   Sir Thomas,
Whither were you a going?
    Lov.   To the cardinal's;
Your lordship is a guest too.
    Cham.   O, 't is true:
This night he makes a supper, and a great one,
To many lords and ladies; there will be
The beauty of this kingdom, I 'll assure you.
    Lov. That churchman bears a bounteous mind indeed,
A hand as fruitful as the land that feeds us;
His dews fall everywhere.
    Cham.   No doubt he 's noble;
He had a black mouth that said other of him.
    Sands. He may, my lord; he has wherewithal; in
      him,
Sparing would show[1] a worse sin than ill doctrine:
Men of his way should be most liberal,
They are set here for examples.
    Cham.   True, they are so;
But few now give so great ones. My barge stays;
Your lordship shall along:—Come, good sir Thomas,
We shall be late else; which I would not be,
For I was spoke to, with sir Henry Guildford,[2]
This night to be comptrollers.
    Sands.   I am your lordship's. [*Ex.*

or lost the vivacity, of youth. Bacon, in his *Sylva Sylvarum*, Cent.
viii., says, 'Horses have, at three years' old, a tooth put forth which
they call the colt's tooth.'
   [1] *Show*] Appear.
   [2] *With Sir Henry, &c.*] To be comptrollers (joint comptroller)
with Sir Henry Guildford. Compare a still customary expression,
exemplified in the *Merchant of Venice*, i. 3, 'I would be friends with
you.'

SCENE IV.—*The Presence-Chamber in* York Place.

Hautboys. A small table under a state for the CARDINAL,
a longer table for the guests. Enter at one door ANNE
BULLEN, *and divers* Lords, Ladies, *and* Gentlewomen, *as
guests; at another door, enter* SIR HENRY GUILDFORD.

Guild. Ladies, a general welcome from his grace
Salutes ye all: This night he dedicates
To fair content, and you : none here, he hopes,
In all this noble bevy, has brought with her
One care abroad : he would have all as merry
As first good company,[1] good wine, good welcome,
Can make good people.   O, my lord, you are tardy;

Enter LORD CHAMBERLAIN, LORD SANDS, *and* SIR THOMAS
LOVELL.

The very thought of this fair company
Clapped wings to me.
    Cham. You are young, sir Harry Guildford :
Sweet ladies, will it please you sit ?   Sir Harry,
Place you that side, I 'll take the charge of this :
His grace is entering.—Nay, you must not freeze ;
Two women placed together makes cold weather :—
My lord Sands, you are one will keep them waking ;
Pray, sit between these ladies.
    Sands.   By my faith,
And thank your lordship.—By your leave, sweet ladies :
                    [*Seats himself between* ANNE BULLEN
                        and another lady.

---

[1] *First good company*] This seems to mean the best good company; but possibly the word *first*, if a genuine reading, signifies *in
the first place.*

If I chance to talk a little wild, forgive me;
I had it from my father.

    Anne.   Was he mad, sir?

    Sands. O, very mad, exceeding mad in love too :
But he would bite none; just as I do now,
He would kiss you twenty with a breath. [*Kisses her.*

    Cham.   Well said, my lord.—
So, now you are fairly seated :—Gentlemen,
The penance lies on you, if these fair ladies
Pass away frowning.

    Sands.   For my little cure,[1]
Let me alone.

    Hautboys. *Enter* CARDINAL WOLSEY, *attended ; and
             takes his state.*

    Wol. You are welcome, my fair guests; that noble
      lady,
Or gentleman, that is not freely merry,
Is not my friend : This, to confirm my welcome;
And to you all good health.   [*Drinks.*

    Sands.   Your grace is noble :—
Let me have such a bowl may hold my thanks,
And save me so much talking.[2]

    Wol.   My lord Sands,
I am beholden to you : cheer your neighbours.
Ladies, you are not merry ;—Gentlemen,
Whose fault is this?

    Sands.   The red wine first must rise
In their fair cheeks, my lord; then we shall have them
Talk us to silence.

    Anne.   You are a merry gamester,
My lord Sands.

    [1] *Cure*] Charge.
    [2] *So much talking*] Returning thanks in words.

Sands.   Yes, if I make my play.[1]
Here 's to your ladyship; and pledge it,[2] madam.
                [*Drum and trumpets within : Chambers* [3]
                    discharged.
Wol.   What 's that?
Cham. Look out there, some of ye.   [*Exit a* Servant.
Wol.   What warlike voice?
And to what end is this?—Nay, ladies, fear not;
By all the laws of war ye are privileged.

                Re-enter Servant.

Cham. How now?   What is 't?
Serv.   A noble troop of strangers;
For so they seem; they have left their barge, and
        landed;
And hither make,[4] as great ambassadors
From foreign princes.
Wol.   Good lord chamberlain,
Go, give them welcome; you can speak the French
        tongue;
And, pray, receive them nobly, and conduct them
Into our presence, where this heaven of beauty
Shall shine at full upon them :—Some attend him.—
                [*Exit* Chamberlain, *attended. All arise, and
                    tables removed.*

---

[1] *If I make my play.*]   I am merry when I gain by what I play.
By *gamester* Anne meant a *maker of diversion;* but Sands, in his
reply, alluded to the more common acceptation of the term.

[2] *Pledge it*]   To pledge a health, in drinking, originally meant, to
taste of the wine first as a guarantee that it contained no poison.
Here Sands desires Anne to acknowledge his pledge.

[3] *Chambers*]   These were small pieces of ordnance used on
festive occasions.

[4] *And hither make, &c.*]   And they come this way, as if they
were, &c.

You have now a broken banquet; but we 'll mend it.
A good digestion to you all : and, once more,
I shower a welcome on you ;—Welcome all.

Hautboys.   Enter the KING, *and twelve others, as maskers,
habited like shepherds, with sixteen torch-bearers ; ushered
by the* Lord Chamberlain.   *They pass directly before the*
CARDINAL, *and gracefully salute him.*

A noble company ! what are their pleasures ?
  Cham. Because they speak no English, thus they prayed
To tell your grace ;—That, having heard by fame
Of this so noble and so fair assembly
This night to meet here, they could do no less,
Out of the great respect they bear to beauty,
But leave their flocks, and, under your fair conduct,[1]
Crave leave to view these ladies, and entreat
An hour of revels with them.
  Wol.   Say, lord chamberlain,
They have done my poor house grace ; for which I pay
          them
A thousand thanks, and pray them take their pleasures.
          [*Ladies chosen for the dance.   The* KING *chooses*
               ANNE BULLEN.
  K. Hen. The fairest hand I ever touched ! O, beauty,
Till now I never knew thee.   [*Music.   Dance.*
  Wol. My lord.
  Cham.   Your grace ?
  Wol. Pray, tell them thus much from me :
There should be one amongst them, by his person,
More worthy this place than myself ; to whom
If I but knew him, with my love and duty
I would surrender it.

----
[1] *Conduct*] Guidance, or introduction.

Cham.   I will, my lord.
                [Cham. *goes to the company, and returns.*
Wol. What say they?
Cham.   Such a one, they all confess,
There is, indeed; which they would have your grace
Find out, and he will take it.[1]
Wol.   Let me see then.—
                [*Comes from his state.*
By all your good leaves, gentlemen; Here I'll make
My royal choice.
        K. Hen.   You have found him,[2] cardinal:
                [*Unmasking.*
You hold a fair assembly; you do well, lord:
You are a churchman, or I'll tell you, cardinal,
I should judge now unhappily.[3]
        Wol.   I am glad
Your grace is grown so pleasant.[4]
        K. Hen.   My lord chamberlain,
Prithee, come hither: What fair lady's that?
        Cham. An't please your grace, Sir Thomas Bullen's
                daughter,
The viscount Rochford,[5] one of her highness' women.
        K. Hen. By heaven, she is a dainty one.—Sweetheart,
I were unmannerly to take you out,
And not to kiss you.—A health, gentlemen.
Let it go round.

        [1] *Take it*] Take your place.
        [2] *You have found him*] Cavendish says the cardinal mistook,
and pitched upon Sir Edward Nevill.
        [3] *Unhappily*] Unfavourably; unpleasantly.
        [4] *Pleasant*] Jocular.
        [5] *The viscount Rochford*] Not, however, created viscount till
after the king had fallen in love with Anne.

Wol. Sir Thomas Lovell, is the banquet ready
I' the privy chamber?
　　Lov.　　　　　　　Yes, my lord.
　　Wol.　　　　　　　　　　Your grace,
I fear, with dancing, is a little heated.
　　K. Hen. I fear, too much.
　　Wol. There 's fresher air, my lord,
In the next chamber.
　　　K. Hen. Lead in your ladies, every one.—Sweet
　　　　partner,
I must not yet forsake you.—Let 's be merry;—
Good my lord cardinal, I have half a dozen healths
To drink to these fair ladies, and a measure [1]
To lead them once again : and then let 's dream
Who 's best in favour.[2]—Let the music knock it.[3]
　　　　　　　　　　　[*Exeunt, with trumpets.*

[1] *A measure*] A dance.
[2] *Best in favour*] The chief beauty. *Favour* is face, or personal appearance.
[3] *Let the music, &c.*] Let the band of music strike up. Drums were used on this occasion. The term *music* often denoted musicians. *See* p. 99, note 2.

ACT II.

SCENE I.—*A Street.*

Enter Two Gentlemen, *meeting.*

1 Gent. Whither away so fast?

2 Gent.   O,—God save you!—
Even to the hall,[1] to hear what shall become
Of the great duke of Buckingham.

1 Gent.   I 'll save you
That labour, sir.   All 's now done, but the ceremony
Of bringing back the prisoner.

2 Gent. Were you there?

1 Gent. Yes, indeed, was I.

2 Gent.   Pray speak what has happened.

1 Gent. You may guess quickly what.

2 Gent.   Is he found guilty?

1 Gent. Yes, truly is he, and condemned upon it.

2 Gent. I am sorry for 't.

1 Gent.   So are a number more.

2 Gent. But, pray, how passed it?

1 Gent. I 'll tell you in a little.[2]   The great duke
Came to the bar; where to his accusations
He pleaded still, not guilty, and alleged
Many sharp reasons to defeat the law.
The king's attorney, on the contrary,

---

[1] *The hall*]   Westminster Hall.
[2] *In a little*]   In few words.

Urged on the examinations, proofs, confessions
Of diver witnesses,—which the duke desired
To have brought, *vivâ voce*, to his face:
At which appeared against him, his surveyor;
Sir Gilbert Peck his chancellor; and John Car,
Confessor to him; with that devil-monk,[1]
Hopkins, that made this mischief.

 2 Gent.   That was he
That fed him with his prophecies?

 1 Gent.   The same.
All these accused him strongly; which he fain
Would have flung from him, but, indeed, he could not:
And so his peers, upon this evidence,
Have found him guilty of high treason. Much
He spoke, and learnedly, for life; but all
Was either pitied in him, or forgotten.

 2 Gent. After all this, how did he bear himself?

 1 Gent. When he was brought again to the bar, to hear
His knell rung out, his judgment, he was stirred
With such an agony, he sweat extremely,
And something spoke in choler, ill and hasty;
But he fell to himself again, and sweetly
In all the rest showed a most noble patience.

 2 Gent. I do not think he fears death.

 1 Gent.   Sure, he does not;
He never was so womanish; the cause
He may a little grieve at.

 2 Gent.   Certainly
The cardinal is the end of this.[2]

 1 Gent.   'T is likely,
By all conjectures: First, Kildare's attainder,

---

[1] *Devil-monk*] So called because he invented lying prophecies to delude Buckingham.

[2] *Is the end of this*] Sought his own end in this.

Then deputy of Ireland ; who removed,
Earl Surrey was sent thither, and in haste too,
Lest he should help his father.

    1 Gent.   That trick of state
Was a deep envious[1] one.

    1 Gent.   At his return,
No doubt, he will requite it. This is noted,
And generally, whoever the king favours
The cardinal instantly will find employment,[2]
And far enough from court too.

    2 Gent.   All the commons
Hate him perniciously, and, o' my conscience,
Wish him ten fathom deep : this duke as much
They love and dote on ; call him bounteous Buckingham,
The mirror of all courtesy.[3]

Enter BUCKINGHAM *from his arraignment ;* Tipstaves *before
him ; the axe with its edge towards him ; halberds on each
side ; accompanied with* SIR THOMAS LOVELL, SIR NICHO-
LAS VAUX, SIR WILLIAM SANDS, *and common people.*

    1 Gent.   Stay there, sir,
And see the noble ruined man you speak of.

    2 Gent. Let 's stand close, and behold him.

    Buck.   All good people,
You that thus far have come to pity me,
Hear what I say, and then go home and lose me

---

   [1] *Envious*] Malicious.

   [2] *This is noted, &c.*] This is observed, and generally too, that
the cardinal will instantly find anyone employment whom the king
favours, &c.

   [3] *The mirror of all courtesy*] The reflecting pattern of all
courtly accomplishments. So Ophelia calls Hamlet 'The glass
of fashion and the mould of form.' *See* the Editor's *Hamlet,* p. 79,
note 1.

I have this day received a traitor's judgment,
And by that name must die : Yet, heaven bear witness,
And, if I have a conscience, let it sink me,
Even as the axe falls, if I be not faithful !
The law I bear no malice for my death,
It has done, upon the premises,[1] but justice ;
But those that sought it I could wish more christians :
Be what they will, I heartily forgive them :
Yet let them look they glory not in mischief,
Nor build their evils [2] on the graves of great men ;
For then my guiltless blood must cry against them.
For further life in this world I ne'er hope,
Nor will I sue, although the king have mercies
More than I dare make faults.[3]   You few that loved me,
And dare be bold to weep for Buckingham,
His noble friends, and fellows, whom to leave
Is only bitter to him, only dying,[4]
Go with me, like good angels, to my end ;
And, as the long divorce of steel [5] falls on me,
Make of your prayers one sweet sacrifice,
And lift my soul to heaven.—Lead on, o' God's name.

Lov. I do beseech your grace, for charity,
If ever any malice in your heart
Were hid against me, now to forgive me frankly.

Buck. Sir Thomas Lovell, I as free forgive you
As I would be forgiven : I forgive all :
There cannot be those numberless offences

---

[1] *The premises*] The *præmissa*, or things put first, the prefatory statement of charges against me.

[2] *Their evils*] Their evil schemes.

[3] *More than I dare, &c.*] More than the faults I dare complain of.

[4] *Is only, &c.*] Is alone bitter to him, alone what constitutes dying.

[5] *The long divorce of steel*] The long separation of the axe.

'Gainst me that I cannot take peace with : [1]
No black envy shall make [2] my grave.
Commend me to his grace ;
And if he speak of Buckingham, pray tell him,
You met him half in heaven : my vows and prayers
Yet are the king's; and, till my soul forsake,
Shall cry for blessings on him : May he live
Longer than I have time to tell [3] his years !
Ever beloved and loving may his rule be !
And, when old time shall lead him to his end,
Goodness and he fill up one monument ! [4]

    Lov. To the water side I must conduct your grace ;
Then give my charge up to Sir Nicholas Vaux,
Who undertakes you to your end.

    Vaux.   Prepare there .
The duke is coming ; see the barge be ready ;
And fit it with such furniture as suits
The greatness of his person.

    Buck.   Nay, sir Nicholas,
Let it alone ; my state [5] now will but mock me.
When I came hither [6] I was lord high constable,
And duke of Buckingham ; now, poor Edward Bohun ; [7]
Yet I am richer than my base accusers,

---

   [1] *Take peace with*] Make peace with. So we have in the early
writers *take a truce* for *make a truce. See* the Editor's *K. John*, p.
42, note 5.

   [2] *Make*] Another reading is *mark.*

   [3] *To tell*] To count.

   [4] *Goodness and he, &c.*] May goodness and his name denote but
one thing on his monument.

   [5] *My state*] The tokens of my rank.

   [6] *When I came hither*] This refers to his coming up from his
palace of Thornbury, in Gloucestershire, to London.

   [7] *Edward Bohun*] Shakspeare was here misled by Holinshed.
The duke's name was Edward Stafford.

That never knew what truth meant: I now seal it;
And with that blood will [1] make them one day groan for 't.
My noble father, Henry of Buckingham,
Who first raised head against usurping Richard,
Flying for succour to his servant Banister,
Being distressed, was by that wretch betrayed,
And without trial fell; God's peace be with him !
Henry the seventh succeeding, truly pitying
My father's loss, like a most royal prince,
Restored me to my honours, and, out of ruins,
Made my name once more noble.   Now his son,
Henry the eighth, life, honour, name, and all
That made me happy, at one stroke has taken
For ever from the world.   I had my trial,
And must needs say, a noble one; which makes me
A little happier [2] than my wretched father:
Yet thus far we are one in fortunes,—Both
Fell by our servants, by those men we loved most;
A most unnatural and faithless service !
Heaven has an end in all: Yet, you that hear me,
This from a dying man receive as certain:
Where you are liberal of your loves and counsels,
Be sure you be not loose; [3] for those you make friends,
And give your hearts to, when they once perceive
The least rub [4] in your fortunes, fall away
Like water from ye, never found again
But where they mean to sink ye.   All good people,
Pray for me ! I must now forsake ye; the last hour
Of my long weary life is come upon me.

[1] *Will*] That will.
[2] *Happier*] More favoured or fortunate.
[3] *Loose*] Unguarded in speech.
[4] *Rub*] Impediment. A *rub* is an obstacle in a bowling alley, that may arrest or turn aside the ball.

Farewell :
And when you would say something that is sad,
Speak how I fell.—I have done ; and God forgive me !

             [*Exeunt* BUCKINGHAM *and Train.*

  1 *Gent.* O, this is full of pity !—Sir, it calls,
I fear, too many curses on their heads
That were the authors.

  2 *Gent.*   If the duke be guiltless,
'T is full of woe: yet I can give you inkling
Of an ensuing evil, if it fall,
Greater than this.

  1 *Gent.*   Good angels keep it from us !
What may it be? You do not doubt my faith, sir ?

  2 *Gent.* This secret is so weighty, 't will require
A strong faith to conceal it.

  1 *Gent.*   Let me have it ;
I do not talk much.

  2 *Gent.*   I am confident ;
You shall,[1] sir : Did you not of late days hear
A buzzing, of a separation
Between the king and Katharine ?

  1 *Gent.*   Yes, but it held not :[2]
For when the king once heard it, out of anger
He sent command to the lord mayor, straight
To stop the rumour, and allay those tongues
That durst disperse it.

  2 *Gent.*   But that slander, sir,
Is found a truth now : for it grows again
Fresher than e'er it was ; and held for certain
The king will venture at it. Either the cardinal,
Or some about him near, have, out of malice
To the good queen, possessed him with a scruple

     [1] *You shall*] You shall have it.
     [2] *It held not*] It did not hold good ; it was contradicted.

That will undo her: To confirm this too,
Cardinal Campeius is arrived, and lately;
As all think, for this business.

   1 *Gent.*   'T is the cardinal;
And merely to revenge him on the emperor,[1]
For not bestowing on him, at his asking,
The archbishopric of Toledo, this is purposed.

   2 *Gent.* I think you have hit the mark: But is 't not
       cruel
That she should feel the smart of this? The cardinal
Will have his will, and she must fall.

   1 *Gent.*   'T is woful.
We are too open here to argue this;
Let 's think [2] in private more.   [*Exeunt.*

     SCENE II.—*An Antechamber in the Palace.*

   '*Enter the* LORD CHAMBERLAIN, *reading a letter.*

Cham.

  'My Lord,—The horses your lordship sent for, with all the care
I had I saw well chosen, ridden, and furnished. They were young
and handsome; and of the best breed in the north. When they
were ready to set out for London, a man of my lord cardinal's, by
commission, and main power, took 'em from me; with this reason,—
His master would be served before a subject, if not before the king ·
which stopped our mouths, sir.'
I fear he will, indeed: Well, let him have them:
He will have all, I think.

    Enter the DUKES OF NORFOLK *and* SUFFOLK.

Nor. Well met, my lord chamberlain.
Cham. Good day to both your graces.

---

  [1] *The emperor*] Charles, the queen's nephew.
  [2] *Think*] Discuss.

Suf. How is the king employed?

Cham. .   I left him private,
Full of sad thoughts and troubles.

Nor.   What 's the cause?

Cham. It seems the marriage with his brother's wife
Has crept too near his conscience.

Suf.   No, his conscience
Has crept too near another lady.

Nor.   'T is so :
This is the cardinal's doing, the king-cardinal :
That blind priest, like the eldest [1] son of fortune,
Turns what he list. [2]   The king will know him one day.

Suf. Pray God he do ! he 'll never know himself else.

Nor. How holily he works in all his business !
And with what zeal ! [3]   For now [4] he has cracked the
          league
Between us and the emperor, the queen's great nephew,
He dives into the king's soul ; and there scatters
Dangers, doubts, wringing of the conscience,
Fears, and despairs ; and all these for his marriage :
And out of all these to restore the king,
He counsels a divorce : a loss of her
That, like a jewel, has hung twenty years
About his neck, yet never lost her lustre :
Of her that loves him with that excellence
That angels love good men with ; even of her
That, when the greatest stroke of fortune falls,
Will bless the king : And is not this course pious ?

Cham. Heaven keep me from such counsel ?   'T is most
          true

[1] *The eldest son*]   The chief heir.
[2] *Turns what he list*]   Turns the wheel to any issue he pleases.
[3] *Zeal*]   Religious fervour.
[4] *Now*)   Now that.

These news are everywhere ; every tongue speaks them,
And every true heart weeps for 't : All that dare
Look into these affairs see this main end,—
The French king's sister.[1] Heaven will one day open
The king's eyes, that so long have slept upon [2]
This bold bad man.

  Suf.   And free us from his slavery.

  Nor. We had need pray,
And heartily, for our deliverance ;
Or this imperious man will work us all
From princes into pages : all men's honours,
Lie like one lump before him, to be fashioned
Into what pitch he please.

  Suf.   For me, my lords,
I love him not, nor fear him ; there 's my creed :
As I am made without him, so I 'll stand,
If the king please ; his curses and his blessings
Touch me alike, they are breath I not believe in.
I knew him, and I know him ; so I leave him
To him that made him proud, the pope.

  Nor.   Let 's in,
And, with some other business, put the king
From these sad thoughts, that work too much upon him :
My lord, you 'll bear us company?

  Cham.   Excuse me,
The king hath sent me other-where ; besides,
You 'll find a most unfit time to disturb him :
Health to your lordships.

  Nor. Thanks, my good lord chamberlain.
        [*Exit* Lord Chamberlain.

---

 [1] *The French king's sister*] The Duchess of Alençon, as the wife
intended for the king by Wolsey.

 [2] *Slept upon*] Been blind to.

NORFOLK *opens a folding-door. The* KING *is discovered sitting, and reading pensively.*

Suf. How sad he looks! sure, he is much afflicted.
K. Hen. Who is there? ha?
Nor.   Pray God, he be not angry.
K. Hen. Who 's there, I say? How dare you thrust
       yourselves
Into my private meditations?
Who am I? ha?
Nor. A gracious king, that pardons all offences
Malice ne'er meant: our breach of duty, this way,
Is business of estate; in which we come
To know your royal pleasure.
     K. Hen.   You are too bold;
Go to; I 'll make ye know your times of business:
Is this an hour for temporal affairs? ha?

Enter WOLSEY *and* CAMPEIUS.

Who 's there? my good lord cardinal?—O my Wolsey,
The quiet of my wounded conscience,
Thou art a cure fit for a king.—You're welcome,
                   ⌊ *To* CAMPEIUS.
Most learned reverend sir, into our kingdom;
Use us, and it:—My good lord, have great care
I be not found a talker.   [*To* WOLSEY.
     Wol.   Sir, you cannot.
I would your grace would give us but an hour
Of private conference.
     K. Hen.   We are busy; go.
                  [*To* NORFOLK *and* SUFFOLK.

Nor. This priest has no pride in him?
Suf.   Not to speak of;
I would not be so sick, though, for his place:
But this cannot continue.   } *Aside.*
Nor.   If it do,
I 'll venture one have-at-him.
Suf.   I another.

[*Exeunt* NORFOLK *and* SUFFOLK.

Wol. Your grace has given a precedent of wisdom
Above all princes, in committing freely
Your scruple to the voice of Christendom:
Who can be angry now? what envy reach you?
The Spaniard, tied by blood and favour to her,
Must now confess, if they have any goodness,
The trial just and noble.   All the clerks,
I mean the learned ones, in christian kingdoms,
Have their free voices;—Rome, the nurse of judgment,
Invited by your noble self, hath sent
One general tongue unto us, this good man,
This just and learned priest, cardinal Campeius:
Whom, once more, I present unto your highness.
    K. Hen. And, once more, in mine arms I bid him wel-
        come,
And thank the holy conclave [1] for their loves;
They have sent me such a man I would have wished for.
    Cam. Your grace must needs deserve all strangers'
        loves,
You are so noble: To your highness' hand
I tender my commission; by whose virtue,
(The court of Rome commanding,) you, my lord
Cardinal of York, are joined with me their servant,
In the unpartial judging of this business.

    [1] *Conclave*] Assembly of cardinals.

D

K. Hen. Two equal¹ men.   The queen shall be acquainted,
Forthwith, for what you come:—Where 's Gardiner ?

Wol. I know your majesty has always loved her
So dear in heart, not to deny her that²
A woman of less place might ask by law,—
Scholars allowed freely to argue for her.

 K. Hen. Ay, and the best she shall have; and my
   favour
To him that does best; God forbid else.   Cardinal,
Prithee call Gardiner to me, my new secretary;
I find him a fit fellow.   [*Exit* WOLSEY.

   Re-enter WOLSEY, *with* GARDINER.

 Wol. Give me your hand : much joy and favour to you;
You are the king's now.

 Gard.   But to be commanded
For ever by your grace, whose hand has raised me. [*Aside.*

 K. Hen. Come hither, Gardiner.

       [*They converse apart.*
 Cam. My lord of York, was not one doctor Pace
In this man's place before him?

 Wol.   Yes, he was.

 Cam. Was he not held a learned man ?

 Wol.   Yes, surely.

 Cam. Believe me, there 's an ill opinion spread, then,
Even of yourself, lord cardinal.

 Wol.   How ! of me ?

 Cam. They will not stick to say you envied him ;
And fearing he would rise, he was so virtuous,

    ¹ *Equal*]   Impartial.
    ² *That*]   That which.

Kept him a foreign man still ;[1] which so grieved him,
That he ran mad, and died.

   Wol.   Heaven's peace be with him !
That 's christian care enough : for living murmurers
There 's places of rebuke.   He was a fool ;
For he would needs be virtuous : That good fellow,[2]
If I command him, follows my appointment ;
I will have none so near else.   Learn this, brother,
We live not to be griped[3] by meaner persons.

   K. Hen. Deliver this with modesty to the queen.
                                  [Exit GARDINER.
The most convenient place that I can think of,
For such receipt of learning, is Blackfriars ;
There ye shall meet about this weighty business :
My Wolsey, see it furnished.   O my lord,
Would it not grieve an able man to leave
So sweet a bedfellow ?   But, conscience, conscience,—
O, 'tis a tender place, and I must leave her.   *[Exeunt.*

      SCENE III.—*An Antechamber in the* Queen's
                   Apartments.

     Enter ANNE BULLEN *and an old* Lady.

   Anne. Not for that, neither :—Here 's the pang that
             pinches :
His highness having lived so long with her : and she
So good a lady, that no tongue could ever
Pronounce dishonour of her ;—by my life,
She never knew harm-doing ;—O now, after

---

   [1] *Kept him a foreign man still*]   Kept him always employed in
embassies abroad, that he might be ' far enough from court.'   Dr.
Pace had occasionally complained of Wolsey to the king.

   [2] *That good fellow*]   Gardiner, the new secretary.

   [3] *Griped*]   Held in check.

So many courses of the sun enthroned,
Still growing in a majesty and pomp,—the which
To leave a thousand-fold more bitter than
'T is sweet at first to acquire,—after this process,[1]
To give her the avaunt! it is a pity
Would move a monster.

  Old L.   Hearts of most hard temper
Melt and lament for her.

  Anne.   O, God's will! much better
She ne'er had known pomp: though it be temporal,
Yet, if that quarrel, fortune,[2] do divorce
It from the bearer, 't is a sufferance,[3] panging
As soul and body's severing.

  Old L.   Alas, poor lady!
She 's a stranger[4] now again.

  Anne.   So much the more
Must pity drop upon her. Verily,
I swear, 't is better to be lowly born,
And range[5] with humble livers in content,
Than to be perked up in a glistering grief,
And wear a golden sorrow.

 [1] *Process*] Process of time.

 [2] *That quarrel, fortune*] No satisfactory interpretation or emendation of the word *quarrel*, in this place, has yet been suggested. With some misgiving, I refer to an old meaning of *quarrel*, viz., argument, cause, or reason, as perhaps applicable here. A contest in which fortune is the quarrel, is an arbitrary one, in which the mere luck of superiority is aimed at, not being founded on any of the technical *causes* specified in the laws of the duello. *See* the Editor's *Macbeth*, p. 5, note 5.

 [3] *A sufferance*] A pain. In *Antony and Cleopatra*, iv. 11, Charmian says, 'The soul and body rive not more in parting, than greatness going off.'

 [4] *A stranger*] A foreigner, a Spaniard.

 [5] *Range*] Rank.

Old L.   .   Our content
Is our best having.[1]

Anne.   I would not be a queen.

Old L. Beshrew me, I would; faith, and so would you,
For all this spice[2] of your hypocrisy:
You, that have so fair parts of woman on you,
Have too a woman's heart: which ever yet
Affected[2] eminence, wealth, sovereignty;
Which, to say sooth, are blessings: and which gifts
(Saving your mincing) the capacity
Of your soft cheveril[4] conscience would receive,
If you might please to stretch it.

Anne.   Nay, good troth,—

Old L. Yes, troth, and troth,—You would not be a
          queen?

Anne. No, not for all the riches under heaven.

Old L. 'T is strange: a three-pence bowed[5] would hire me,
Old as I am, to queen it:[6] But, I pray you,
What think you of a duchess? have you limbs
To bear that load of title?

Anne.   No, in truth.

Old L. Then you are weakly made: Pluck off a little;[7]

---

[1] *Having*] Possession.

[2] *Spice*] Form or specimen. Lat. *species*. So in Chaucer's
Parson's Tale, 'And yet is there a privy spice of pride;' 'This sin
hath many spices.' *See* the Editor's *Coriolanus*, p. 125, note 4.

[2] *Affected*] Desired; had affection towards.

[4] *Cheveril*] Kid-skin; soft glove leather. So in *Romeo and
Juliet*, ii. 4, 'Here 's a wit of cheveril, that stretches from an inch
narrow to an ell broad.'

[5] *A three-pence bowed*] Bent or crooked coin was accounted lucky
money.

[6] *To queen it*] To assume the office of queen.

[7] *Pluck off a little*] Suppose we reduce a little the load of title;
what say you to a countess?

I would not be a young count in your way,
For more than blushing comes to.

Anne. How you do talk!
I swear again, I would not be a queen
For all the world.

Old L. In faith, for little England
You 'd venture an emballing:[1] I myself
Would for Carnarvonshire, although there 'longed
No more to the crown but that. Lo, who comes here?

Enter the LORD CHAMBERLAIN.

Cham. Good morrow, ladies. What were 't worth to
know
The secret of your conference?

Anne. My good lord,
Not your demand![2] it values not your asking:
Our mistress' sorrows we were pitying.

Cham. It was a gentle business, and becoming
The action of good women: there is hope
All will be well.

Anne. Now I pray God, amen!

Cham. You bear a gentle mind, and heavenly blessings
Follow such creatures. That you may, fair lady,
Perceive I speak sincerely, and high note 's
Ta'en of your many virtues, the king's majesty
Commends his good opinion to you, and
Does purpose honour to you no less flowing
Than marchioness of Pembroke; to which title
A thousand pound a-year, annual support,
Out of his grace he adds.

[1] *An emballing*] A coronation; part of that ceremony consisting
in placing a sceptre in the queen's right hand, and a globe or *ball* in
her left.

[2] *Not your demand*] It were not worth your demand.

Anne.　　　　　　　I do not know
What kind of my obedience I should tender;
More than my all is nothing; nor my prayers
Are not words duly hallowed, nor my wishes
More worth than empty vanities; yet prayers, and wishes,
Are all I can return.　Beseech your lordship,
Vouchsafe to speak my thanks, and my obedience,
As from a blushing handmaid to his highness;
Whose health and royalty I pray for.
　　Cham.　　　　　　　　　Lady,
I shall not fail to approve the fair conceit [1]
The king hath of you.—I have perused her well;　[*Aside.*
Beauty and honour in her are so mingled,
That they have caught the king; and who knows yet,
But from this lady may proceed a gem
To lighten all this isle! [2]—I 'll to the king,
And say, I spoke with you.
　　Anne.　　　　　　My honoured lord.
　　　　　　　　　[*Exit* Lord Chamberlain.
　Old L. Why, this it is; see, see !
I have been begging sixteen years in court,
(Am yet a courtier beggarly), nor could
Come pat betwixt too early and too late,
For any suit of pounds: and you (O fate !)
A very fresh-fish [3] here (fie, fie upon
This compelled fortune !) have your mouth filled up
Before you open it.

　[1] *To approve the fair conceit*]　To justify the good opinion.
　[2] *To lighten, &c.*]　'Some wonderful properties relative to an imaginary gem, called a carbuncle, formed part of the popular creed. It was supposed to be the most transparent of all the precious stones. and to possess a native intrinsic lustre so powerful as to illuminate the atmosphere to a considerable distance around it.'　Drake's *Shakspeare and his Times.*
　[3] *Fresh-fish*]　A fish just landed; a new comer.

Anne.   This is strange to me.

Old L. How tastes it? is it bitter? forty pence, no.[1]
There was a lady once[2] ('t is an old story),
That would not be a queen, that would she not,
For all the mud in Egypt:—Have you heard it?

Anne. Come, you are pleasant.[3]

Old L.   With your theme, I could
O'ermount the lark. The marchioness of Pembroke!
A thousand pounds a-year! for pure respect;
No other obligation: By my life,
That promises more thousands: Honour's train
Is longer than his foreskirt. By this time,
I know, your back will bear a duchess;—Say,
Are you not stronger than you were?

Anne.   Good lady,
Make yourself mirth with your particular fancy,
And leave me out on't. Would I had no being,
If this salute my blood[4] a jot; it faints me
To think what follows.
The queen is comfortless, and we forgetful
In our long absence: Pray, do not deliver
What here you have heard, to her.

Old L.   What do you think me?   [*Exeunt.*

SCENE IV.—*A Hall in* Blackfriars.

Trumpets, sennet,[5] *and cornets. Enter two* Vergers, *with
short silver wands; next them, Two* Scribes, *in the habits*

---

[1] *Forty-pence, no*] I wager forty pence it is not. The sum here
mentioned was half a noble.

[2] *There was a lady once*] This sarcastically refers to Anne herself.

[3] *Pleasant*] Jocose.

[4] *Salute my blood*] Excite my spirits.

[5] *Sennet*] This word is probably from the Italian *segno* or *segnata*,
meaning *giving a signal.*

of doctors; after them, the ARCHBISHOP OF CANTERBURY
alone; after him, the BISHOPS OF LINCOLN, ELY, ROCHESTER,
and SAINT ASAPH ; *next them, with some small distance,
follows a* Gentleman *bearing the purse, with the great seal,
and a cardinal's hat; then Two* Priests, *bearing each a
silver cross; then a* Gentleman-Usher *bare-headed, accompanied with a* Sergeant at Arms, *bearing a silver mace;
then Two* Gentlemen, *bearing two great silver pillars ;
after them, side by side, the Two* CARDINALS WOLSEY *and*
CAMPEIUS; *Two* Noblemen *with the sword and mace.*
[*Then enter the* KING *and* QUEEN, *and their Trains.*] *The*
KING *takes place under the cloth of state; the two* CAR-
DINALS *sit under him as judges. The* QUEEN *takes place
at some distance from the* KING. *The* BISHOPS *place themselves on each side the court, in manner of a consistory ;
below them, the* Scribes. *The* Lords *sit next the* BISHOPS.
The Crier *and the rest of the* Attendants *stand in conve-
nient order about the stage.*

Wol. Whilst our commission[1] from Rome is read,
Let silence be commanded.
   K. Hen.   What's the need?
It hath already publicly been read,[2]
And on all sides the authority allowed ;
You may then spare that time.
   Wol.   Be 't so :—Proceed.
   Scribe. Say, Henry king of England, come into the
      court.
   Crier. Henry king of England, &c.

---

  [1] *Commission*] This word is here quadrisyllabic. Shakspeare
often makes the terminations *-sion* and *-tion* dissyllabic at the end
of a line, but rarely does so in the middle.
  [2] *It hath already, &c.*] It had been read at a previous meeting
of the court.

K. Hen. Here.

Scribe. Say, Katharine queen of England, come into the court.

Crier. Katharine queen of England, &c.

[*The* QUEEN *makes no answer, rises out of her chair, goes about the court, comes to the* KING, *and kneels at his feet; then speaks.*

Q. Kath. Sir, I desire you do me right and justice;
And to bestow your pity on me: for
I am a most poor woman, and a stranger,
Born out of your dominions; having here
No judge indifferent,[1] nor no more assurance
Of equal friendship and proceeding. Alas, sir,
In what have I offended you? what cause
Hath my behaviour given to your displeasure,
That thus you should proceed to put me off,
And take your good grace from me? Heaven witness,
I have been to you a true and humble wife,
At all times to your will conformable:
Ever in fear to kindle your dislike,
Yea, subject to your countenance; glad, or sorry,
As I saw it inclined. When was the hour,
I ever contradicted your desire,
Or made it not mine too? Or which of your friends
Have I not strove to love, although I knew
He were mine enemy? What friend of mine
That had to him derived your anger, did I
Continue in my liking? nay, gave notice
He was from thence discharged? Sir, call to mind
That I have been your wife, in this obedience,
Upwards of twenty years, and have been blest
With many children by you: If, in the course

---

[1] *Indifferent*] Impartial.

And process of this time, you can report,
And prove it too, against mine honour aught,
My bond to wedlock, or my love and duty,
Against your sacred person,—in God's name,
Turn me away ; and let the foul'st contempt
Shut door upon me, and so give me up
To the sharpest kind of justice.   Please you, sir,
The king, your father, was reputed for
A prince most prudent, of an excellent
And unmatched wit and judgment : Ferdinand,
My father, king of Spain, was reckoned one
The wisest prince, that there had reigned by many
A year before : it is not to be questioned
That they had gathered a wise council to them
Of every realm, that did debate this business,
Who deemed our marriage lawful : Wherefore I humbly
Beseech you, sir, to spare me, till I may
Be by my friends in Spain advised ; whose counsel
I will implore ; if not, i' the name of God,
Your pleasure be fulfilled !

Wol.   You have here, lady,
(And of your choice), these reverend fathers ; men
Of singular integrity and learning.
Yea, the elect of the land, who are assembled
To plead your cause : It shall be therefore bootless,
That longer you desire the court ; [1] as well
For your own quiet, as to rectify
What is unsettled in the king.

   Cam.   His grace
Hath spoken well, and justly : Therefore, madam,
It 's fit this royal session do proceed ;
And that, without delay, their arguments
Be now produced, and heard.

----

[1] *That longer, &c.*]   That you desire the court to delay proceedings.

Q. Kath.   Lord cardinal,
To you I speak.

Wol.   Your pleasure, madam?

Q. Kath.   Sir,
I am about to weep; but, thinking that
We are a queen, (or long have dreamed so), certain
The daughter of a king, my drops of tears
I 'll turn to sparks of fire.

Wol.   Be patient yet.

Q. Kath. I will, when you are humble; nay, before,
Or God will punish me.   I do believe,
Induced by potent circumstances,[1] that
You are mine enemy; and make my challenge [2]
You shall not be my judge: for it is you
Have blown this coal betwixt my lord and me,
Which God's dew quench?—Therefore, I say again,
I utterly abhor, yea, from my soul
Refuse you for my judge: [3] whom, yet once more,
I hold my most malicious foe, and think not
At all a friend to truth.

Wol.   I do profess [4]
You speak not like yourself; who ever yet
Have stood to charity, and displayed the effect
Of disposition gentle, and of wisdom
O'ertopping woman's power.   Madam, you do me wrong:

---

[1] *Induced, &c.*]   Being brought to such belief by strongly convincing circumstances.

[2] *Challenge*]   The word is here used as a law term, and has reference to the custom of a criminal refusing a juryman by saying, 'I challenge him.'

[3] *I utterly abhor, &c.*]   *Abhor* and *refuse* are the words in Holinshed; and, as Blackstone observes in reference to this passage, are technical terms of the Canon Law, corresponding to the Latin words *Detestor* and *Recuso.*

[4] *Profess*)   Assert.

I have no spleen against you ; nor injustice
For you, or any : how far I have proceeded,
Or how far further shall, is warranted
By a commission from the consistory,
Yea, the whole consistory of Rome.   You charge me
That I have blown this coal : I do deny it :
The king is present : if it be known to him
That I gainsay my deed, how may he wound,
And worthily, my falsehood ? yea, as much
As you have done my truth.   But if he know
That I am free of your report, he knows
I am not of your wrong.[1]   Therefore in him
It lies to cure me : and the cure is, to
Remove these thoughts from you : The which before
His highness shall speak in, I do beseech
You, gracious madam, to unthink your speaking,
And to say so no more.
   Q. Kath.   My lord, my lord,
I am a simple woman, much too weak
To oppose your cunning.   You are meek, and humble-
      mouthed ;
You sign [2] your place and calling, in full seeming
With [3] meekness and humility : but your heart
Is crammed with arrogancy, spleen, and pride.
You have, by fortune, and his highness' favours,
Gone slightly o'er low steps : [4] and now are mounted
Where powers are your retainers : [5] and your words,
Domestics to you, serve your will, as 't please

---

[1] *Of your wrong*]   Free of your wrong ; free of injury from you.
[2] *Sign*]   Signify outwardly.
[3] *In full seeming with, &c.*]   With all the appearance of.
[4] *Gone slightly, &c.*]   Gone gently upwards by easy ascent.
[5] *Powers are your retainers*]   Nobles are in your retinue.

Yourself pronounce their office.¹   I must tell you,
You tender more your person's honour than
Your high profession spiritual : That² again
I do refuse you for my judge ; and here,
Before you all, appeal unto the pope,
To bring my whole cause 'fore his holiness,
And to be judged by him.

        [*She curtsies to the* KING, *and offers to depart.*

  Cam.   The queen is obstinate,
Stubborn to justice, apt to accuse it, and
Disdainful to be tried by it; 't is not well.
She's going away.

  K. Hen. Call her again.

  Crier. Katharine queen of England, come into the court.

  Grif. Madam, you are called back.

  Q. Kath. What need you note it ? pray you, keep your
    way :
When you are called, return.—Now the Lord help,
They vex me past my patience !—pray you, pass on :
I will not tarry : no, nor ever more,
Upon this business, my appearance make
In any of their courts.

        [*Exeunt* QUEEN, GRIFFITH, *and her other*
           Attendants.

  K. Hen.   Go thy ways, Kate :
That man i' the world who shall report he has
A better wife, let him in nought be trusted,
For speaking false in that : Thou art, alone,
(If thy rare qualities, sweet gentleness,
Thy meekness saint-like, wife-like government—
Obeying in commanding,—and thy parts

  ¹ *As 't please yourself, &c.*] According to every business you
charge them with.
  ² *That*] So that; wherefore.

Sovereign and pious else, could speak thee out),[1]
The queen of earthly queens :—She is noble born ;
And, like her true nobility, she has
Carried herself towards me.

    Wol.   Most gracious sir,
In humblest manner I require your highness,
That it shall please you to declare, in hearing
Of all these ears, (for where I am robbed and bound,
There must I be unloosed ; although not there
At once and fully satisfied,)[2] whether ever I
Did broach this business to your highness ; or
Laid any scruple in your way, which might
Induce you to the question on 't ? or ever
Have to you,—but with thanks to God for such
A royal lady,—spoke one the least word that might
Be to the prejudice of her present state,
Or touch of her good person ?

    K. Hen.   My lord cardinal
I do excuse [3] you ; yea, upon mine honour,
I free you from 't.   You are not to be taught [4]
That you have many enemies, that know not
Why they are so, but, like to village curs,
Bark when their fellows do : by some of these
The queen is put in anger.   You are excused :
But will you be more justified ? you ever
Have wished the sleeping of this business ; never
Desired it to be stirred : but oft have hindered, oft,
The passages [5] made toward it :—on my honour,

    [1] *Could speak thee out*]   Might describe thee fully ; might all be told.

    [2] *Satisfied*]   Indemnified.

    [3] *Excuse*]   Acquit.

    [4] *You are not to be taught*]   You do not need to be informed.

    [5] *Passages*]   Approaches.   The usual meaning of this word in the old writers is *occurrences*, things as they *come to pass*.

I speak [1] my good lord cardinal to this point,[2]
And thus far clear him.   Now, what moved me to 't,
I will be bold, with time, and your attention :—
Then mark the inducement.   Thus it came ;—give heed
       to 't :
My conscience first received a tenderness,
Scruple, and prick, on certain speeches uttered
By the bishop of Bayonne, then French ambassador ;
Who had been hither sent on the debating
A marriage, 'twixt the duke of Orleans and
Our daughter Mary : I' the progress of this business,
Ere a determinate resolution, he
(I mean the bishop) did require a respite ;
Wherein he might the king his lord advertise
Whether our daughter were legitimate,
Respecting this our marriage with the dowager,
Sometime our brother's wife.   This respite shook
The bosom of my conscience, entered me,
Yea, with a splitting power, and made to tremble
The region of my breast ; which forced such way,
That many mazed considerings did throng,
And pressed in with this caution.   First, methought,
I stood not in the smile of heaven ; who had
Commanded nature, that my lady's womb,
If it conceived a male child by me, should
Do no more offices of life to 't, than
The grave does to the dead : for her male issue
Or [3] died where they were made, or shortly after
This world had aired them : Hence I took a thought
This was a judgment on me ; that my kingdom,

---

[1] *I speak*]   I describe.   So in iii. 1, ' Let me speak myself ;' and
in iv. 2, ' No other speaker of my living actions.'
[2] *To this point*]   Thus far.
[3] *Or*]   Either.

Well worthy the best heir o' the world, should not
Be gladded in 't by me : Then follows, that
I weighed the danger which my realms stood in
By this my issue's fail : and that gave to me
Many a groaning throe. Thus hulling [1] in
The wild sea of my conscience, I did steer
Toward this remedy, whereupon we are
Now present here together ; that 's to say,
I meant to rectify my conscience,—which
I then did feel full sick, and yet not well,—
By all the reverend fathers of the land,
And doctors learn'd. First, I began in private
With you, my lord of Lincoln ; you remember
How under my oppression I did reek,
When I first moved you.

    Lin.   Very well, my liege.

    K. Hen. I have spoke long ; be pleased yourself to say
How far you satisfied me.

    Lin.   So please your highness,
The question did at first so stagger me,—
Bearing [2] a state of mighty moment in 't,
And consequence of dread,—that I committed
The daring'st counsel which I had, to doubt ; [3]
And did entreat your highness to this course,
Which you are running here.

    K. Hen.   I then moved you,
My lord of Canterbury ; and got your leave
To make this present summons :—Unsolicited

---

   [1] *Hulling*] Floating, like a dismasted vessel. So Milton, speaking of Adam's vision, says he 'saw the ark hull on the flood,' *P. L.* xi. 840.

   [2] *Bearing*] Importing ; involving.

   [3] *I committed, &c.*] I committed to doubt, repressed under hesitation, the most forward opinion of my own mind.

I left no reverend person in this court;
But by particular consent proceeded,
Under your hands and seals.   Therefore, go on;
For no dislike i' the world against the person
Of the good queen, but the sharp thorny points
Of my allegèd reasons, drive this forward:
Prove but our marriage lawful, by my life,
And kingly dignity, we are contented
To wear our mortal state to come with her,
Katharine our queen, before the primest creature
That 's paragoned o' the world.[1]

   Cam.   So please your highness,
The queen being absent, 't is a needful fitness,
That we adjourn this court till further day:
Meanwhile must be an earnest motion
Made to the queen, to call back her appeal
She intends unto his holiness.   *[They rise to depart.*

   K. Hen.   I may perceive,   *[Aside.*
These cardinals trifle with me: I abhor
This dilatory sloth, and tricks of Rome.
My learn'd and well-belovèd servant, Cranmer,[2]
Prithee, return! with thy approach, I know,
My comfort comes along.   Break up the court:
I say, set on.   *[Exeunt in manner as they entered.*

---

[1] *Paragoned*] Extolled as a paragon.
[2] *Cranmer*] He was at this time absent on an embassy.

ACT III.

SCENE I.— *Palace at* Bridewell. *A Room in the* Queen's *Apartment.*

The QUEEN, *and some of her* Women, *at work.*

Q. Kath. Take thy lute, wench : my soul grows sad with troubles :
Sing, and disperse them if thou canst : leave working.

SONG.

Orpheus[1] with his lute made trees,
And the mountain-tops that freeze,
  Bow themselves, when he did sing :
To his music, plants and flowers
Ever sprung ; as sun and showers
  There had made a lasting spring.

Everything that heard him play,
Even the billows of the sea,
  Hung their heads and then lay by.
In sweet music is such art,
Killing care[2] and grief of heart
  Fall asleep, or, hearing, die.

Enter a Gentleman.

Q. Kath. How now ?

---

[1] *Orpheus*] One of the early poets and musicians of Greece, of whom it was fabled that mountains and trees moved in cadence to his song, rivers paused in their courses to listen to it, &c.

[2] *Killing care*] That killing care.

Gent. An 't please your grace, the two great cardinals
Wait in the presence.[1]
Q. Kath.   Would they speak with me?
Gent. They will'd me say so, madam.
Q. Kath.   Pray their graces
To come near.   [*Exit* Gent.] What can be their business
With me, a poor weak woman, fallen from favour?
I do not like their coming.   Now I think on 't,
They should be good men; their affairs as righteous:
But all hoods make not monks.[2]

Enter WOLSEY *and* CAMPEIUS.

Wol.   Peace to your highness!
Q. Kath. Your graces find me here part of a housewife;
I would be all, against the worst may happen.
What are your pleasures with me, reverend lords?
Wol. May it please you, noble madam, to withdraw
Into your private chamber, we shall give you
The full cause of our coming.
Q. Kath.   Speak it here;
There 's nothing I have done yet, o' my conscience,
Deserves a corner: Would all other women
Could speak this with as free a soul as I do!
My lords, I care not, (so much I am happy[3]
Above a number,) if my actions
Were tried by every tongue, every eye saw them,
Envy and base opinion set against them,
I know my life so even:[4] If your business

---

[1] *The presence*] The presence chamber.
[2] *All hoods, &c.*] A reference to the Latin proverb, 'Cucullus non
facit monachum.'
[3] *Happy*] Fortunate.
[4] *Even*] Consistent; upright.

Seek me out, and that way I am wife in,[1]
Out with it boldly :   Truth loves open dealing.

   Wol.   *Tanta est ergà te mentis integritas, regina serenis-*
        sima,—[2]

   Q. Kath.   O good my lord, no Latin ;
I am not such a truant since my coming,
As not to know the language I have lived in :
A strange tongue makes my cause more strange, suspicious ;
Pray speak in English : here are some will thank you,
If you speak truth, for their poor mistress' sake ;
Believe me she has had much wrong : Lord cardinal,
The willingest sin[3] I ever yet committed
May be absolved in English.

   Wol.   Noble lady,
I am sorry my integrity should breed,—
And service to his majesty and you,—
So deep suspicion where all faith was meant.
We come not by the way of accusation,
To taint that honour every good tongue blesses ;
Nor to betray you any way to sorrow ;
You have too much, good lady : but to know
How you stand minded in the weighty difference
Between the king and you ; and to deliver,
Like free and honest men, our just opinions,
And comforts to your cause.

   Cam.   Most honoured madam, ·

   [1] *Seek me out, &c.*]   Seek to investigate my character, and the
nature of my marriage.

   [2] *Tanta est, &c.*]   So great is our integrity of purpose towards
you, most serene princess.   Katharine was able to read and write
Latin in her childhood, and she was through life desirous of im-
provement in that language.   She chiefly employed her knowledge
of Latin in the diligent perusal of the Scriptures, a fact which Eras-
mus affirms.—Strickland's *Lives of the Queens.*

   [3] *The willingest sin*]   The most presumptuous sin.

My lord of York,—out of his noble nature,
Zeal and obedience he still bore your graces;[1]
Forgetting, like a good man, your late censure
Both of his truth and him, (which was too far,[2])—
Offers, as I do, in a sign of peace,
His service and his counsel.

    Q. Kath.   To betray me.   [*Aside.*
My lords, I thank you both for your good wills;
Ye speak like honest men; pray God, ye prove so!
But how to make ye suddenly an answer,
In such a point of weight, so near mine honour,
(More near my life, I fear,) with my weak wit,
And to such men of gravity and learning,
In truth, I know not. I was set at work
Among my maids; full little, God knows, looking
Either for such men, or such business.
For her sake that I have been,[3] (for I feel
The last fit[4] of my greatness,) good your graces,[5]
Let me have time, and counsel, for my cause;
Alas! I am a woman, friendless, hopeless.

    Wol. Madam, you wrong the king's love with these fears;
Your hopes and friends are infinite.

    Q. Kath.   In England
But little for my profit;[6] Can you think, lords,
That any Englishman dare give me counsel?
Or be a known friend, 'gainst his highness' pleasure,

---

[1] *He still bore, &c.*]   He ever bore towards the king and you.
[2] *Was too far*]   Was going too far.
[3] *For her sake, &c.*]   For the sake of her that I have been.
[4] *Fit*]   Sense or impression.
[5] *Your graces*]   These two words form a title qualified by the adjective *good*, as in the expressions, 'good my lord,' 'dear my liege,' 'sweet my child.'
[6] *But little, &c.*]   They are of but little avail.

(Though he be grown so desperate to be honest,) [1]
And live a subject? [2]   Nay, forsooth ; my friends,
They that must weigh out [3] my afflictions,
They that my trust must grow to,[4] live not here :
They are, as all my other comforts, far hence,
In mine own country, lords.

 Cam.   I would your grace
Would leave your griefs, and take my counsel.

 Q. Kath.   How, sir ?

 Cam. Put your main cause into the king's protection ;
He's loving and most gracious ; 't will be much
Both for your honour better, and your cause ;
For, if the trial of the law o'ertake you,
You 'll part [5] away disgraced.

 Wol.   He tells you rightly.

 Q. Kath. Ye tell me what ye wish for both, my ruin
Is this your christian counsel? out upon ye !
Heaven is above all yet ; there sits a Judge
That no king can corrupt.

 Cam.   Your rage mistakes us.

 Q. Kath. The more shame for ye ; holy men I thought ye,
Upon my soul, two reverend cardinal virtues ; [6]
But cardinal sins, and hollow hearts, I fear ye : [7]
Mend them, for shame, my lords.   Is this your comfort ?
The cordial that ye bring a wretched lady ?

---

 [1] *Though he be grown, &c.*] Notwithstanding his having become
so desperately anxious to be honest,—in relation to our marriage.

 [2] *A subject*] Regarded as a loyal subject.

 [3] *Weigh out*] Estimate and urge.

 [4] *Grow to*] Be attached to.

 [5] *Part*] Depart. Fr. *partir.*

 [6] *Cardinal virtues*] This sarcastic use of the word *cardinal* has
reference to the ancient recognition of justice, prudence, temperance,
and fortitude, as the cardinal or chief virtues.

 [7] *I fear ye*] I fear ye are.

A woman lost among ye, laughed at, scorned?
I will not wish ye half my miseries;
I have more charity: but say,[1] I warned ye;
Take heed, for heaven's sake, take heed, lest at once
The burden of my sorrows fall upon ye.

Wol. Madam, this is a mere distraction;
You turn the good we offer into envy.[2]

Q. Kath. Ye turn me into nothing: Woe upon ye,
And all such false professors! Would ye have me
(If you have any justice, any pity;
If ye be anything but churchmen's habits)
Put my sick cause into his hands that hates me?
Alas! he has banished me his bed already;
His love, too long ago: I am old, my lords,
And all the fellowship I hold now with him
Is only my obedience. What can happen
To me above this wretchedness? all your studies[3]
Make me a curse like this.

Cam.   Your fears are worse—

Q. Kath. Have I lived thus long—(let me speak[4]
          myself,
Since virtue finds no friends)—a wife, a true one?
A woman (I dare say without vain-glory)
Never yet branded with suspicion?
Have I with all my full affections
Still met the king? loved him next heaven? obeyed him?
Been, out of fondness, superstitious to him?
Almost forgot my prayers to content him?
And am I thus rewarded? 't is not well, lord
Bring me a constant woman to her husband,

---

[1] *But say, &c.*] But I will say that I, &c.
[2] *Envy*] Malice.
[3] *Studies*] Deliberations and endeavours.
[4] *Speak*] Describe.

One that ne'er dreamed a joy beyond his pleasure;
And to that woman, when she has done most,
Yet will I add an honour,—a great patience.[1]

Wol. Madam, you wander from the good we aim at.

Q. Kath. My lord, I dare not make myself so guilty
To give up willingly that noble title
Your master wed me to: nothing but death
Shall e'er divorce my dignities.

Wol.   Pray, hear me.

Q. Kath. Would I had never trod this English earth,
Or felt the flatteries that grow upon it!
Ye have angels' faces,[2] but heaven knows your hearts.
What will become of me now, wretched lady?
I am the most unhappy woman living.
Alas! poor wenches, where are now your fortunes?

                              [*To her* Women.

Shipwracked upon a kingdom, where no pity,
No friends, no hope; no kindred weep for me;
Almost no grave allowed me:—Like the lily,
That once was mistress of the field and flourished,
I'll hang my head and perish.

Wol.   If your grace
Could but be brought to know our ends are honest,
You'd feel more comfort: why should we, good lady,
Upon what cause, wrong you? alas! our places,
The way of our profession is against it;
We are to cure such sorrows, not to sow them.
For goodness' sake, consider what you do;
How you may hurt yourself, ay, utterly

---

[1] *To that woman, &c.*] To that woman's highest merit I will,
in order to describe myself, add this further merit, a great patience.

[2] *Ye have angels' faces*] Ye English have angels' faces. This
may be, as some suppose, in allusion to the old story of Pope
Gregory calling the *Angles* fair as *angels*.

E

Grow from the king's acquaintance,[1] by this carriage.
The hearts of princes kiss obedience,
So much they love it; but to stubborn spirits
They swell, and grow as terrible as storms.
I know you have a gentle, noble temper,
A soul as even as a calm : Pray think us
Those we profess, peace-makers, friends, and servants.

   Cam. You 'll find it so. You wrong your virtues
With these weak women's fears. A noble spirit,
As yours was put into you, ever casts
Such doubts, as false coin, from it. The king loves you,—
Beware you lose it[2] not : For us, if you please
To trust us in your business, we are ready
To use our utmost studies in your service.

   Q. Kath. Do what ye will, my lords : And, pray, for-
       give me.
If I have used myself[3] unmannerly ;
You know I am a woman, lacking wit
To make a seemly answer to such persons.
Pray, do my service to his majesty :
He has my heart yet, and shall have my prayers,
While I shall have my life. Come, reverend fathers,
Bestow your counsels on me : she now begs,
That little thought, when she set footing here,
She should have bought her dignities so dear. [*Exeunt.*

---

   [1] *Grow from, &c.*] Be disowned by the king.
   [2] *It*] With this pronominal reference to the noun implied in the
verb *loves*, compare *Othello*, iii. 4, 'And bid me, when my fate would
have me *wive*, to give it *her.*'
   [3] *Used myself*] Deported or conducted myself; behaved.

SCENE II.—*Antechamber to the* King's *Apartment.*

Enter the DUKE OF NORFOLK, *the* DUKE OF SUFFOLK, *the*
EARL OF SURREY, *and the* Lord Chamberlain.

Nor. If you will now unite in your complaints,
And force them with a constancy, the cardinal
Cannot stand under them : If you omit
The offer of this time, I cannot promise
But that you shall sustain more new disgraces,
With these you bear already.
  Sur.   I am joyful
To meet the least occasion, that may give me
Remembrance of my father-in-law, the duke,
To be revenged on him.
  Suf.   Which of the peers
Have uncontemned gone by him, or at least
Strangely neglected ? [1] when did he regard
The stamp of nobleness in any person
Out of himself ?
  Cham. My lords, you speak your pleasures :
What he deserves of you and me I know ;
What we can do to him, (though now the time
Gives way to us,) I much fear. If you cannot
Bar his access to the king, never attempt
Anything on him ; for he hath a witchcraft
Over the king in his tongue.
  Nor.   O, fear him not ;
His spell in that is out : [2] the king hath found
Matter against him, that for ever mars

---

[1] *Strangely neglected*] Neglected as if unknown to him.
[2] *Is out*] Has completed its period.

The honey of his language. No, he's settled,[1]
Not to come off, in his displeasure.

Sur.   Sir,
I should be glad to hear such news as this
Once every hour.

Nor.   Believe it, this is true;
In the divorce, his contrary proceedings
Are all unfolded; wherein he appears,
As I would wish mine enemy.

Sur.   How came
His practices[2] to light?

Suf. .   Most strangely.

Sur.   O, how, how?

Suf. The cardinal's letter to the Pope miscarried,
And came to the eye o' the king: wherein was read,
How that the cardinal did entreat his holiness
To stay the judgment o' the divorce: For if
It did take place, 'I do,' quoth he, 'perceive,
My king is tangled in affection to
A creature of the queen's, lady Anne Bullen.

Sur. Has the king this?

Suf.   Believe it.

Sur.   Will this work?

Cham. The king in this perceives him, how he coasts
And hedges his own way.[3] But in this point
All his tricks founder, and he brings his physic
After his patient's death; the king already
Hath married the fair lady.

---

[1] *He is settled*] He is fixed in the king's displeasure, never to
get out of it. There is here an allusion to a stranded vessel which
cannot be floated off again.

[2] *Practices*] Devices.

[3] *Coasts and hedges, &c.*] Moves stealthily by coast and hedge
in his own course.

Sur.   Would he had !

Suf. May you be happy in your wish, my lord !
For, I profess, you have it.

Sur.   Now all joy
Trace the conjunction ! [1]

Suf.   My amen to 't !

Nor.   All men's !

Suf. There 's order given for her coronation
Marry, this is yet but young, and may be left
To some ears unrecounted.[2]—But, my lords,
She is a gallant creature, and complete
In mind and feature : I persuade me, from her
Will fall some blessing to this land, which shall
In it be memorized.[3]

Sur.   But, will the king
Digest[4] this letter of the cardinal's ?
The Lord forbid !

Nor.   Marry, amen !

Suf.   .   No, no ;
There be more wasps that buzz about his nose,
Will make this sting the sooner.   Cardinal Campeius
Is stolen away to Rome ; hath ta'en no leave ;
Has left the cause o' the king unhandled ; and
Is posted, as the agent of our cardinal,
To second all his plot.   I do assure you,
The king cried, ha ! at this.

---

[1] *All joy trace, &c.*] May all joy be prognosticated by the astro-
logical tracing of this conjunction. When two planets were in the
same sign of the zodiac, their aspect was called Conjunction. In
2 *K. Henry IV.* ii. 4, the prince says, ' Saturn and Venus this year
in conjunction : what says the almanac to that ? '

[2] *To some ears, &c.*] Wolsey did not yet know of it.

[3] *Memorized*] Made memorable.

[4] *Digest*] Put up with ; forgive.

Cham.   Now, God incense him,
And let him cry ha, louder !
    Nor.   But, my lord,
When returns Cranmer ?
    Suf. He is returned, in his opinions; [1] which
Have satisfied the king for his divorce,
Together with all famous colleges
Almost in Christendom : shortly, I believe,
His second marriage shall be published, and
Her coronation.   Katharine no more
Shall be called queen; but princess dowager,
And widow to prince Arthur.
    Nor.   This same Cranmer's
A worthy fellow, and hath ta'en much pain
In the king's business.
    Suf.   He has; and we shall see him,
For it, an archbishop.
    Nor.   So I hear.
    Suf.   'T is so.

Enter WOLSEY *and* CROMWELL.

    Nor.   Observe, observe, he's moody.
    Wol. The packet, Cromwell, gave it you the king ?
    Crom. To his own hand, in his bedchamber.
    Wol. Looked he o' the inside of the paper ?
    Crom.   Presently
He did unseal them : and the first he viewed,
He did it with a serious mind; a heed
Was in his countenance : You he bade
Attend him here this morning.
    Wol.   Is he ready
To come abroad ?
    Crom.   I think, by this he is.

---

[1] *In his opinions*] In his own unaltered opinions.

Wol. Leave me a while.—   [*Exit* CROMWELL.
It shall be to the duchess of Alençon,
The French king's sister : he shall marry her.—
Anne Bullen ! No; I 'll no Anne Bullens for him :
There is more [1] in it than fair visage.—Bullen !
No, we 'll no Bullens.—Speedily I wish
To hear from Rome.—The marchioness of Pembroke !
    Nor. He 's discontented.
    Suf.   May be, he hears the king
Does whet his anger to him.
    Sur.   Sharp enough,
Lord, for thy justice !
    Wol. The late queen's gentlewoman; a knight's daughter,
To be her mistress' mistress ! the queen's queen ;—
This candle burns not clear; 't is I must snuff it;
Then, out it goes.—What though I know her virtuous,
And well deserving? yet I know her for
A spleeny Lutheran; and not wholesome to
Our cause, that she should lie i' the bosom of
Our hard-ruled [2] king. Again, there is sprung up
An heretic, an arch one,—Cranmer ; one
Hath [3] crawled into the favour of the king,
And is his oracle.

[1] *More*] Matter of more importance.

[2] *Hard-ruled.*] Hard-ruling ; wilful. Wolsey feared that Anne
might inspire the king with Lutheran sentiments, which he would
wilfully maintain against the Church. Cavendish says, 'Forsooth
it is a world to consider the desirous will of wilful princes, when
they be set and earnestly bent to have their wills fulfilled; and above
all things there is nothing that maketh them more wilful than carnal
love.'—*Ruled*, for *ruling*, or *having ruled*, is an instance of a use of
the past participle very common with Shakspeare. Thus, in *Cymbeline*, v. 4, we have 'To make my gift, the more delayed, *delighted*;'
and in *Othello*, i. 3, ' If virtue no *delighted* beauty lack.'

[3] *Hath*] That hath.

Nor.   He is vexed at something.

Suf. I would 't were something that would fret the string,
The master-cord [1] of his heart !

     Enter the KING, *reading a schedule ; and* LOVELL.

Suf.   The king, the king.

K. Hen. What piles of wealth hath he accumulated
To his own portion ! and what expense by the hour
Seems to flow from him ! How, i' the name of thrift,
Does he rake this together ?—Now, my lords,
Saw you the cardinal ?

    Nor.   My lord, we have
Stood here observing him : Some strange commotion
Is in his brain : he bites his lip, and starts ;
Stops on a sudden, looks upon the ground,
Then, lays his finger on his temple ; straight,
Springs out into fast gait ; then, stops again,
Strikes his breast hard ; and anon, he casts
His eye against the moon : in most strange postures
We have seen him set himself.

    K. Hen.   It may well be ;
There is a mutiny in his mind. This morning
Papers of state he sent me to peruse,
As I required : And wot you what I found
There ; on my conscience, put unwittingly ?
Forsooth, an inventory, thus importing,—
The several parcels of his plate, his treasure,
Rich stuffs, and ornaments of household ; which
I find at such proud rate, that it out-speaks
Possession of a subject.[2]

---

[1] *The master-cord*] Wolsey's pride is meant.
[2] *Out-speaks, &c.*] Bespeaks more than a subject may properly possess.

Nor.   It 's heaven's will:
Some spirit put this paper in the packet
To bless your eye withal.
　K. Hen.   If we did think
His contemplation were above the earth,
And fixed on spiritual object, he should still
Dwell in his musings : but, I am afraid,
His thinkings are below the moon, not worth
His serious considering.[1]

　　　　[*He takes his seat, and whispers* LOVELL, *who
　　　　　　　goes to* WOLSEY.

　Wol.   Heaven forgive me!—[2]
Ever God bless your highness!
　K. Hen.   Good my lord,
You are full of heavenly stuff, and bear[3] the inventory
Of your best graces in your mind; the which
You were now running o'er; you have scarce time
To steal from spiritual leisure a brief span
To keep your earthly audit :[4] Sure, in that
I deem you an ill husband;[5] and am glad
To have you therein my companion.
　Wol.   Sir,
For holy offices I have a time; a time
To think upon the part of business which
I bear i' the state; and nature does require
Her times of preservation, which, perforce,

---

[1] *Not worth, &c.*] And ought not to engross his mind so seriously.
[2] *Heaven forgive me!*] Lovell has made Wolsey aware of the king's presence, whereupon Wolsey asks pardon for not having observed his majesty.
[3] *Bear, &c.*] Bear in your mind, are remembering, &c.
[4] *To keep your earthly audit*] To examine and regulate your earthly affairs.
[5] *An ill husband*] A bad manager.

I her frail son, amongst my brethren mortal,
Must give my tendance to.

K. Hen.   You have said well.

Wol. And ever may your highness yoke together,
As I will lend you cause,[1] my doing well
With my well-saying !

K. Hen.   'T is well said again ;
And 't is a kind of good deed to say well :
And yet words are no deeds.   My father loved you :
He *said* he did ; and with his *deed* did crown [2]
His word upon you.   Since I had my office,
I have kept you next my heart ; have not alone
Employed you where high profits might come home,
But pared my present havings, to bestow
My bounties upon you.

Wol.   What should this mean ?

Sur. The Lord increase this business !   [*Aside.*

K. Hen.   Have I not made you
The prime man of the state ?   I pray you, tell me,
If what I now pronounce you have found true :
And, if you may confess it, say withal,
If you are bound to us, or no.   What say you ?

Wol. My sovereign, I confess, your royal graces,
Showered on me daily, have been more than could
My studied purposes requite ; which went
Beyond all man's endeavours :—my endeavours
Have ever come too short of my desires,
Yet filed [3] with my abilities.   Mine own ends
Have been mine so, that evermore they pointed
To the good of your most sacred person, and

---

[1] *As I will lend you cause*]   As I will give you reason to do.

[2] *Crown*]   Honour; fulfil.   Similarly, in *Macbeth*, iv. 1, 'To crown my thoughts with acts.'

[3] *Filed*]   Kept pace.

The profit of the state. For your great graces
Heaped upon me, poor undeserver, I
Can nothing render but allegiant thanks ;
My prayers to heaven for you ; my loyalty,
Which ever has, and ever shall be growing,
Till death, that winter, kill it.

    K. Hen.   Fairly answered ;
A loyal and obedient subject is
Therein illustrated : The honour of it
Does pay the act of it ; as, i' the contrary,
The foulness is the punishment. I presume
That, as my hand has opened bounty to you,
My heart dropped love, my power rained honour, more
On you than any ; so your hand and heart,
Your brain, and every function of your power,
Should, notwithstanding that your bond of duty,[1]
As 't were in love's particular,[2] be more,
To me, your friend, than any.[3]

    Wol.   I do profess
That for your highness' good I ever laboured
More than mine own ; that am, have, and will be,[4]
Though all the world should crack their duty [5] to you,

[1] *Notwithstanding that your bond of duty*] Independently of that
general bond of duty which is imposed on you as a subject.

[2] *In love's particular*] In individual personal attachment.

[3] *Than any*] Than to any other.

[4] *That am, &c.*] Such a one I am, have been, and will be. We
have here an instance of Shakspeare's frequent disregard of gram-
matical accuracy. He has exemplified such inaccuracy in the preceding speech of Wolsey, where the cardinal says his loyalty ' ever
has and ever shall be growing.' Compare *Troilus and Cressida,* i.
3, where Agamemnon says—

      ' And may that soldier a mere recreant prove,
        That means not, hath not, or is not, in love.'

[5] *Crack their duty*] Snap their bond of duty.

And throw it from their soul : though perils did
Abound, as thick as thought could make them, and
Appear in forms more horrid ; yet my duty,
As doth a rock against the chiding flood,
Should the approach of this wild river break,
And stand unshaken yours.

   K. Hen.   'T is nobly spoken :
Take notice, lords, he has a loyal breast,
For you have seen him open 't.—Read o'er this ;
                        [*Giving him papers.*
And after, this : and then to breakfast, with
What appetite you have.

               Exit KING, *frowning upon* CARDINAL WOLSEY ;
               the Nobles *throng after him, smiling, and*
               whispering.

   Wol.   What should this mean ?
What sudden anger 's this ? how have I reaped it ?
He parted frowning from me, as if ruin
Leaped from his eyes : so looks the chaféd lion
Upon the daring huntsman that has galled him ;
Then makes him nothing.   I must read this paper :
I fear, the story of his anger.—'T is so :
This paper has undone me : 'T is the account
Of all that world of wealth I have drawn together
For mine own ends ; indeed, to gain the popedom,
And fee my friends in Rome.   O negligence,
Fit for a fool to fall by !   What cross devil
Made me put this main secret in the packet
I sent the king ?   Is there no way to cure this,
No new device to beat this from his brains ?
I know 't will stir him strongly ; Yet I know
A way, if it take right, in spite of fortune
Will bring me off again.   What 's this ?—To the Pope ?
The letter, as I live, with all the business

I writ to his holiness. Nay then, farewell !
I have touched the highest point of all my greatness ;
And, from that full meridian of my glory,
I haste now to my setting. I shall fall
Like a bright exhalation in the evening,
And no man see me more.

Re-enter the DUKES OF NORFOLK [1] *and* SUFFOLK, *the* EARL OF
  SURREY, *and the* Lord Chamberlain.

 Nor. Hear the king's pleasure, cardinal: who commands
   you
To render up the great seal presently
Into our hands ; and to confine yourself
To Asher-house, my lord of Winchester's, [2]
Till you hear further from his highness.
 Wol.   Stay,
Where 's your commission, lords ? words cannot carry
Authority so weighty.
 Suf.   Who dares cross them,
Bearing the king's will from his mouth expressly ?
 Wol. Till I find more than will, or words, to do it,
(I mean, your malice, [3]) know, officious lords,
I dare, and must deny it. Now I feel
Of what coarse metal ye are moulded,—envy.
How eagerly ye follow my disgraces,
As if it fed ye ! and how sleek and wanton
Ye appear in everything may bring my ruin !

 [1] *Norfolk*] The duke of Norfolk, here introduced, had been dead
some years ; his son, here called the earl of Surrey, was now duke,
and was the person who with Suffolk came to demand the great seal.
 [2] *Asher-house*] Esher, near Hampton Court, Surrey. Esher
House was a residence of the Bishop of Winchester, and Wolsey
himself now held that see.
 [3] *I mean, &c.*] I mean your malicious will and words.

Follow your envious courses, men of malice;
You have christian warrant for them,[1] and, no doubt,
In time will find their fit rewards. That seal
You ask with such a violence, the king,
(Mine, and your master,) with his own hand gave me:
Bade me enjoy it, with the place and honours,
During my life, and, to confirm his goodness,
Tied it by letters patent:[2] Now, who 'll take it?

   Sur. The king, that gave it.

   Wol.   It must be himself then.

   Sur. Thou art a proud traitor, priest.

   Wol.   Proud lord, thou liest;
Within these forty hours Surrey durst better
Have burnt that tongue than said so.

   Sur.   Thy ambition,
Thou scarlet sin,[3] robbed this bewailing land
Of noble Buckingham, my father-in-law:
The heads of all thy brother cardinals
With thee, and all thy best parts bound together,
Weighed not a hair of his. Plague of your policy!
You sent me deputy for Ireland:
Far from his succour, from the king, from all
That might have mercy on the fault thou gavest him;
Whilst your great goodness, out of holy pity,
Absolved him with an axe.

---

[1] *You have christian warrant, &c.*] This is said ironically.

[2] *Patent*] This word, in the expression *letters patent*, means *open*, openly conferring a right or privilege.

[3] *Scarlet sin.*] An allusion to Wolsey's usual dress and the distinguishing colour of a cardinal's hat, and at the same time either to St. John's description of the woman of sin, Rev. xvii. 3, 4, or to the colour by which heinous iniquity is represented in Isaiah, i. 18. Wolsey was called by his enemies 'the red man.' In 1 *K. Henry VI.* i. 3, Glo'ster calls Cardinal Beaufort a 'scarlet hypocrite.'

Wol.   This, and all else
This talking lord can lay upon my credit,[1]
I answer is most false.   The duke by law
Found his deserts : how innocent I was
From any private malice in his end,
His noble jury and foul cause can witness.
If I loved many words, lord, I should tell you,
You have as little honesty as honour ;
That I, in the way of loyalty and truth
Toward the king, my ever royal master,
Dare mate a sounder man than Surrey can be,
And all that love his follies.
    Sur.   By my soul,
Your long coat, priest, protects you ! thou shouldst feel
My sword i' the life-blood of thee else.—My lords,.
Can ye endure to hear this arrogance ?
And from this fellow ?   If we live thus tamely
And be thus jaded [2] by a piece of scarlet,
Farewell nobility ; let his grace go forward,
And dare us with his cap, like larks.[3]
    Wol.   All goodness
Is poison to thy stomach.
    Sur.   Yes, that goodness
Of gleaning all the land's wealth into one,

---

[1] *Lay upon my credit*]   Lay to my charge.

[2] *Jaded*]   Made jades of ; disparaged.

[3] *Dare us, &c.*]   To *dare*, in bird-catching, signified to amaze or confound.   Steevens says, 'It is well known that the hat of a cardinal is scarlet, and that one of the methods of *daring* larks was by small mirrors fastened on scarlet cloth, which engaged the attention of those birds while the fowler drew his net over them.'   In *King Henry V.* iv. 2, the Constable of France says—

'For our approach shall so much dare the field,
    That England shall couch down in fear, and yield.'

Into your own hands, cardinal, by extortion;
The goodness of your intercepted packets,
You writ to the pope, against the king: your goodness,
Since you provoke me, shall be most notorious.
My lord of Norfolk, as you are truly noble,
As you respect the common good, the state
Of our despised nobility, our issues,
Who, if he live, will scarce be gentlemen,—
Produce the grand sum of his sins, the articles
Collected from his life :—I 'll startle you.

Wol. How much, methinks, I could despise this man,
But that I am bound in charity against it !

Nor. Those articles, my lord, are in the king's hand :
But, thus much, they are foul ones.

Wol.   So much fairer,
And spotless, shall mine innocence arise,
When the king knows my truth.

Sur.   This cannot save you :
I thank my memory, I yet remember
Some of these articles ; and out they shall.
Now, if you can blush, and cry guilty, cardinal,
You 'll show a little honesty.

Wol.   Speak on, sir ;
I dare your worst objections : If I blush,
It is, to see a nobleman want manners.

Suf. I 'd rather want those than my head. Have at
        you.

(1) First, that, without the king's assent or knowledge,
You wrought to be a legate ; by which power [1]
You maimed the jurisdiction of all bishops.

(2) *Nor.* Then, that in all you writ to Rome, or else

---

[1] *By which power*]   Thus introducing an authority whereby.

To foreign princes, *Ego et Rex meus* [1]
Was still inscribed; in which you brought the king
To be your servant.

(3) Suf.   Then, that, without the knowledge
Either of king or council, when you went
Ambassador to the emperor, you made bold
To carry into Flanders the great seal.

(4,) Sur. Item, you sent a large commission
To Gregory de Cassalis, to conclude,
Without the king's will, or the state's allowance,
A league between his highness and Ferrara. [2]

(5) Suf. That, out of mere ambition, you have caused
Your holy hat to be stamped on the king's coin.

(6) Sur. Then, that you have sent innumerable substance
(By what means got, I leave to your own conscience,)
To furnish Rome, and to prepare the ways
You have for dignities; to the mere undoing
Of all the kingdom./ Many more there are;
Which, since they are of you, and odious,
I will not taint my mouth with.

Cham.   O, my lord,
Press not a falling man too far; 'tis virtue:
His faults lie open to the laws; let them,
Not you, correct him. My heart weeps to see him
So little of his great self. [3]

Sur.   I forgive him.

Suf. Lord cardinal, the king's further pleasure is,—
Because all those things, you have done of late,
By your power legatine within this kingdom,

---

[1] *Ego et Rex meus*] The precedence of *ego* was defended by Wolsey as being a Latin usage.

[2] *Ferrara*] The duke of Ferrara.

[3] *So little, &c.*] So small a part of what he has been.

Fall into the compass of a *præmunire,*— [1]
That therefore such a writ be sued against you;
To forfeit all your goods, lands, tenements,
Chattels, and whatsoever, and to be
Out of the king's protection :—This is my charge.

   Nor. And so we'll leave you to your meditations
How to live better. For your stubborn answer,
About the giving back the great seal to us,
The king shall know it, and, no doubt, shall thank you.
So fare you well, my little good lord cardinal.

                         [*Exeunt all but* WOL:

   Wol. So farewell to the little good you bear me.
Farewell, a long farewell, to all my greatness!
This is the state [2] of man : To-day he puts forth
The tender leaves of hope, to-morrow blossoms,
And bears his blushing honours thick upon him :
The third day comes a frost, a killing frost ;
And,—when he thinks, good easy man, full surely
His greatness is a ripening,—nips his root,
And then he falls, as I do. I have ventured,
Like little wanton boys that swim on bladders,
This many summers in a sea of glory ;
But far beyond my depth : my high-blown pride
At length broke under me ; and now has left me,
Weary and old with service, to the mercy
Of a rude stream, that must for ever hide me.
Vain pomp and glory of this world, I hate ye ;
I feel my heart new opened : O, how wretched
Is that poor man that hangs on princes' favours !

   [1] *A præmunire*] This word is a corruption of *præmoneri.* This
species of writ is so called from the first words of it directing that
the person be *forewarned* respecting the offence of introducing foreign
authority in England.
   [2] *The state*] The earthly dignity.

There is, betwixt that smile he would aspire to,
That sweet aspect of princes, and his ruin,
More pangs and fears than wars or women have ;
And when he falls, he falls like Lucifer,
Never to hope again.—[1]

Enter CROMWELL, *amazedly.*

                    Why, how now, Cromwell ?
Crom. I have no power to speak, sir.
Wol.   What, amazed [2]
At my misfortunes ? can thy spirit wonder
A great man should decline ?   Nay, an you weep,
I am fallen indeed.
Crom.   How does your grace ?
Wol.   Why, well ;
Never so truly happy,[3] my good Cromwell.
I know myself now ; and I feel within me
A peace above all earthly dignities,
A still and quiet conscience.   The king has cured me,
I humbly thank his grace ; and from these shoulders,
These ruined pillars, out of pity, taken
A load would sink a navy, too much honour:
O, 't is a burden, Cromwell, 't is a burden
Too heavy for a man that hopes for heaven.
    Crom. I am glad your grace has made that right use of it.
    Wol. I hope I have : I am able now, methinks,
(Out of a fortitude of soul I feel,)
To endure more miseries, and greater far,
Than my weak-hearted enemies dare offer.
What news abroad ?

---

[1] *Never to hope again*] Compare this with the third and fourth lines of the speech.
[2] *Amazed*] Confounded.
[3] *Happy*] Fortunate.

Crom.   The heaviest, and the worst,
Is your displeasure with the king.
     Wol.   God bless him!
     Crom. The next is, that sir Thomas More is chosen
Lord chancellor in your place.
     Wol.   That 's somewhat sudden:
But he 's a learnèd man.   May he continue
Long in his highness' favour, and do justice
For truth's sake and his conscience'; that his bones,
When he has run his course, and sleeps in blessings,
May have a tomb of orphans' tears wept on them!
What more?
     Crom. That Cranmer is returned with welcome,—
Installed lord archbishop of Canterbury.
     Wol. That 's news indeed.
                    Last, that the lady Anne,
Whom the king hath in secrecy long married,
This day was viewed in open,[1] as his queen,
Going to chapel; and the voice is now
Only about her coronation.
     Wol. There was the weight that pulled me down.   O
          Cromwell,
The king has gone beyond me; all my glories
In that one woman I have lost for ever:
No sun shall ever usher forth mine honours,
Or gild again the noble troops that waited
Upon my smiles.   Go, get thee from me, Cromwell;
I am a poor fallen man, unworthy now
To be thy lord and master: Seek the king;
That sun, I pray, may never set!   I have told him

---

[1] *Orphans' tears, &c.*] Tears of grateful sorrow shed by orphans
whom he has befriended.   The Lord Chancellor is the general
guardian of orphans.

[2] *In open*] An imitation of the Latin *in aperto*.

What, and how true thou art: he will advance thee;
Some little memory of me will stir him,
(I know his noble nature,) not to let
Thy hopeful service perish too : Good Cromwell,
Neglect him not; make use [1]. now, and provide
For thine own future safety.
    Crom.   O, my lord,
Must I then leave you ?   Must I needs forego
So good, so noble, and so true a master ?
Bear witness, all that have not hearts of iron,
With what a sorrow Cromwell leaves his lord !
The king shall have my service ; but my prayers
For ever, and for ever, shall be yours.
    Wol. Cromwell, I did not think to shed a tear
In all my miseries; but thou hast forced me,
Out of thy honest truth, to play the woman.
Let 's dry our eyes : and thus far hear me, Cromwell ;
And,—when I am forgotten, as I shall be,
And sleep in dull cold marble, where no mention
Of me more must be heard of,—say, I taught thee ;
Say, Wolsey,—that once trod the ways of glory,
And sounded all the depths and shoals of honour,—
Found thee a way, out of his wrack, to rise in,
A sure and safe one, though thy master missed it.
Mark but my fall, and that that ruined me :
Cromwell, I charge thee, fling away ambition ;
By that sin fell the angels ; how can man then,
The image of his Maker,[2] hope to win by 't ?
Love thyself last : cherish those hearts that hate thee,
Corruption wins not more than honesty.

    [1] *Use*] Interest; so called as being payment for the use of
money.
    [2] *The image of his Maker.*] The pertinence of this notion here
is not very apparent.

Still in thy right hand carry gentle peace,[1]
To silence envious tongues. Be just, and fear not.
Let all the ends thou aim'st at be thy country's,
Thy God's, and truth's; then if thou fall'st, O Cromwell,
Thou fall'st a blessed martyr. Serve the king;
And,—Prithee, lead me in : .
There take an inventory of all I have,
To the last penny; 't is the king's : my robe
And my integrity to heaven, is all
I dare now call mine own. O Cromwell, Cromwell,
Had I but served my God with half the zeal
I served [2] my king, he would not in mine age
Have left me naked to mine enemies.

 Crom. Good sir, have patience.

 Wol.   So I have. Farewell
The hopes of court ! my hopes in heaven do dwell. [*Exeunt.*

---

[1] *Carry gentle peace*] An allusion to the ivory or silver rod, sur-
mounted by the dove or bird of peace, carried at processions.

[2] *The zeal I served*] The zeal with which I served. Grammati-
cal imperfection of this kind is very common in Shakspeare. Compare *Merchant of Venice*, ii. 6, 'Who riseth from a feast with that
keen appetite that he sits down?'—and *Othello*, i. 3, 'What drugs,
what charms, &c, I won his daughter.'

ACT IV.

SCENE I.—*A Street in* Westminster.

Enter Two Gentlemen, *meeting.*

1 Gent. You are well met once again.

2 Gent.   And so are you.

1 Gent. You come to take your stand here, and behold
The lady Anne pass from her coronation?

2 Gent. 'T is all my business. At our last encounter,
The duke of Buckingham came from his trial.

1 Gent. 'T is very true : but that time offered sorrow :
This, general joy.

2 Gent.   'T is well : the citizens,
I am sure, have shown at full their royal minds,
(As, let them have their rights,[1] they are ever forward,)
In celebration of this day with shows,
Pageants, and sights of honour.

1 Gent.   Never greater,
Nor, I 'll assure you, better taken,[2] sir.

2 Gent. May I be bold to ask what that contains,
That paper in your hand?

1 Gent.   Yes; 't is the list
Of those that claim their offices this day,
By custom of the coronation.
The duke of Suffolk is the first, and claims

---

[1] *Let them have, &c.*] To give them their due.
[2] *Taken*] Received; welcomed.

To be high steward ; next, the duke of Norfolk,
He to be earl marshal : you may read the rest.

2 Gent. I thank you, sir; had I not known those customs,
I should have been beholden to your paper.
But, I beseech you, what 's become of Katharine,
The princess dowager ? how goes her business ?

1 Gent. That I can tell you too.   The archbishop
Of Canterbury, accompanied with other
Learned and reverend fathers of his order,
Held a late court at Dunstable, six miles off
From Ampthill, where the princess lay ; [1] to which
She was often cited by them, but appeared not :
And, to be short, for not-appearance, and
The king's late scruple, by the main assent
Of all these learned men she was divorced,
And the late marriage made of none effect :
Since which she was removed to Kimbolton,
Where she remains now, sick.

2 Gent.   Alas, good lady !—   [*Trumpets.*
The trumpets sound : stand close, the queen is coming.

THE ORDER OF THE PROCESSION.

A lively flourish of Trumpets : then, enter,

1. *Two Judges.*
2. *Lord Chancellor, with the purse and mace before him.*
3. *Choristers singing.*   [Music.
4. *Mayor of London bearing the mace.   Then Garter, in
    his coat of arms, and, on his head, a gilt copper
    crown.*
5. *Marquis Dorset, bearing a sceptre of gold, on his head
    a demi-coronal of gold.   With him, the Earl of*

---

[1] *Lay*] Lodged ; resided.

> *Surrey, bearing the rod of silver with the dove,*
> *crowned with an earl's coronet. Collars of SS.*[1]

6. *Duke of Suffolk, in his robe of estate, his coronet on*
   his head, bearing a long white wand, as high-
   steward. With him, the Duke of Norfolk, with
   the rod of marshalship, a coronet on his head.
   Collars of SS.

7. *A canopy borne by four of the Cinque-ports;* [2] *under*
   it, the Queen in her robe; in her hair richly
   adorned with pearl, crowned. On each side of
   her, the Bishops of London and Winchester.

8. *The old Duchess of Norfolk, in a coronal of gold,*
   wrought with flowers, bearing the Queen's train.

9. *Certain Ladies or Countesses, with plain circlets of*
   gold without flowers.

2 Gent. A royal train, believe me.—These I know;—
Who 's that that bears the sceptre?

1 Gent.   Marquis Dorset:
And that the earl of Surrey, with the rod.

2 Gent. A bold brave gentleman: and that should be
The duke of Suffolk.

1 Gent.   'T is the same; high-steward.

2 Gent. And that my lord of Norfolk?

1 Gent.   Yes.

2 Gent.   Heaven bless thee!
                        [*Looking on the* QUEEN.

---

[1] *Collars of SS.*] A collar of Esses, probably so called from the
S-shaped links of the chain-work, was a badge of equestrian nobility.
It was united in front by two portcullises with a rose pendent, and
sometimes had ornaments between the Esses. The origin of this
mark of knighthood is unknown.

[2] *Cinque-ports*] Barons of the Cinque-ports. The five ports were
Dover, Hastings, Hythe, Romney, and Sandwich; to which were
afterwards added, Rye and Winchilsea. Their jurisdiction was
vested in barons for the better protection of the English coast.

F

Thou hast the sweetest face I ever looked on.—
Sir, as I have a soul, she is an angel.

    1 *Gent.*   They that bear
The cloth of honour over her, are four barons
Of the Cinque ports.

    2 *Gent.* Those men are happy ; and so are all are near
        her.
I take it, she that carries up the train
Is that old noble lady, duchess of Norfolk.

    1 *Gent.* It is ; and all the rest are countesses..

    2 *Gent.* Their coronets say so. These are stars, indeed. -
        [*Exit Procession, with a great flourish of trumpets.*

Enter a Third Gentleman.

    1 *Gent.* God save you, sir ! where have you been
        broiling ?

    3 *Gent.* Among the crowd i' the abbey ; where a finger
Could not be wedged in more ; I am stifled
With the mere rankness of their joy.

    2 *Gent.* You saw the ceremony ?

    3 *Gent.* That I did.

    1 *Gent.* How was it ?

    3 *Gent.* Well worth the seeing.

    2 *Gent.* Good sir, speak it [1] to us.

    3 *Gent.* As well as I am able. The rich stream
Of lords and ladies, having brought the queen
To a prepared place in the choir,[2] fell off
A distance from her : while her grace sat down
To rest a while, some half an hour, or so,
In a rich chair of state, opposing freely
The beauty of her person to the people :—

   [1] *Speak it*] Describe it. *See* p. 64, note 1.
   [2] *The choir*] That part of the cathedral corresponding to the
chancel of a parish church.

Believe me, sir, she is the goodliest woman
That ever wedded man :—which when the people
Had the full view of, such a noise arose
As the shrouds make at sea in a stiff tempest,
As loud, and to as many tunes : hats, cloaks,—
Doublets, I think,—flew up : and had their faces
Been loose, this day they had been lost. Such joy
I never saw before. No man living
Could say, ' This is my wife,' there ; all were woven
So strangely in one piece.[1]

 2 Gent.   But, what followed ?

 3 Gent. At length her grace rose, and with modest paces
Came to the altar : where she kneeled, and, saint-like,
Cast her fair eyes to heaven, and prayed devoutly,
Then rose again, and bowed her to the people :
When by the archbishop of Canterbury
She had all the royal makings of a queen ;
As holy oil, Edward Confessor's crown,
The rod, and bird of peace, and all such emblems,
Laid nobly on her ; which performed, the choir,
With all the choicest music [2] of the kingdom,
Together sung *Te Deum*. So she parted,[3]
And with the same full state paced back again
To York-place, where the feast is held.

 1 Gent.   Sir,
You must no more call it York-place, that is past :
For, since the cardinal fell, that title 's lost ;
'T is now the king's, and called Whitehall.

 3 Gent.   I know it ;

---

 [1] *All were woven, &c.*] All the dresses were so strangely blended
as it were in one piece.
 [2] *Music*] Musicians. A band of music was often called *music*.
 [3] *Parted*] Departed.

But 't is so lately altered, that the old name
Is fresh about me.

 2 Gent.   What two reverend bishops
Were those that went on each side of the queen ?

 3 Gent. Stokesly and Gardiner; the one, of Winchester,
(Newly preferred from the king's secretary,) [1]
The other, London.

 2 Gent.   He of Winchester
Is held no great good lover of the archbishop's,
The virtuous Cranmer.

 3 Gent. ·   All the land knows that :
However, yet there 's no great breach ; when it comes,
Cranmer will find a friend will not shrink from him.

 2 Gent. Who may that be, I pray you ?

 3 Gent.   Thomas Cromwell ;
A man in much esteem with the king, and truly
A worthy friend.—The king
Has made him master o' the jewel-house,
And one, already, of the privy-council.

 2 Gent. He will deserve more.

 3 Gent.   Yes, without all doubt,
Come, gentlemen, ye shall go my way, which
Is to the court, and there ye shall be my guests ;
Something I can command. [2] As I walk thither
I 'll tell ye more.

 Both. You may command us, sir. [*Exeunt.*

---

[1] *The king's secretary*] The office of king's secretary.

[2] *Something I can command.*] I have something in my power to entertain you.

SCENE II.—Kimbolton.

Enter KATHARINE, *Dowager, sick ; led between* GRIFFITH
and PATIENCE.

Grif. How does your grace ?

Kath.   O, Griffith, sick to death :
My legs, like loaden branches, bow to the earth,
Willing to leave their burden : reach a chair ;—
So ;—now, methinks, I feel a little ease.
Didst thou not tell me, Griffith, as thou leds't me,
That the great child of honour, cardinal Wolsey,
Was dead ?

Grif.   Yes, madam ; but I think your grace,
Out of the pain you suffered, gave no ear to 't.

Kath. Prithee, good Griffith, tell me how he died :
If well, he stepped before me, happily,
For my example.

Grif.   Well, the voice goes,[1] madam :
For after the stout earl Northumberland
Arrested him at York, and brought him forward
(As a man sorely tainted) to his answer,
He fell sick suddenly, and grew so ill,
He could not sit his mule.

Kath.   Alas, poor man !

Grif. At last, with easy roads,[2] he came to Leicester,
Lodged in the abbey ; where the reverend abbot,
With all his convent, honourably received him ;
To whom he gave these words,—' O father abbot,
An old man, broken with the storms of state,
Is come to lay his weary bones among ye ;

---

[1] *Well, the voice goes*] Report says that he died well.
[2] *Roads*] Journeys.

Give him a little earth for charity!'
So went to bed: where eagerly his sickness
Pursued him still; and, three nights after this,
About the hour of eight, (which he himself
Foretold should be his last,) full of repentance,
Continual meditations, tears, and sorrows,
He gave his honours to the world again,
His blessed part to heaven, and slept in peace.

   Kath. So may he rest; his faults lie gently on him!
Yet thus far, Griffith, give me leave to speak him,
And yet with charity:—He was a man
Of an unbounded stomach,[1] ever ranking
Himself with princes; one, that by suggestion
Tied all the kingdom:[2] simony was fair play;
His own opinion was his law: I' the presence
He would say untruths; and be ever double,
Both in his words and meaning: He was never,
But where he meant to ruin, pitiful;
His promises were, as he then was, mighty;
But his performance, as he is now, nothing.
Of his own body he was ill,[3] and gave
The clergy ill example.

   Grif.   Noble madam,
Men's evil manners live in brass; their virtues
We write in water. May it please your highness
To hear me speak his good now?

---

  [1] *Stomach*] Pride.

  [2] *By suggestion tied, &c.*] By an under-working policy bound the
whole kingdom to him. *Tithed,* as some think, may have been
Shakspeare's word, and seems to agree better with the corresponding
passage in Holinshed, where it is said, 'He counted himself equal
with princes, and by crafty suggestion gat into his hands innumerable treasure.'

  [3] *Of his own body, &c.*] In his own person he was sensual.

Kath.   Yes, good Griffith;
I were malicious else.
Grif.   This cardinal,
Though from a humble stock, undoubtedly
Was fashioned to much honour from his cradle.
He was a scholar, and a ripe and good one;
Exceeding wise, fair spoken, and persuading:
Lofty and sour to them that loved him not;
But, to those men that sought him,[1] sweet as summer.
And though he were unsatisfied[2] in getting,
(Which was a sin), yet in bestowing, madam,
He was most princely: Ever witness for him
Those twins of learning that he raised in you,—[3]
Ipswich, and Oxford! one of which fell with him,
Unwilling to outlive the good that did it;
The other, though unfinished, yet so famous,
So excellent in art, and still so rising,
That Christendom shall ever speak his virtue.
His overthrow heaped happiness[4] upon him;
For then, and not till then, he felt himself,
And found the blessedness of being little:
And, to add greater honours to his age
Than man could give him, he died fearing God.
Kath. After my death I wish no other herald,
No other speaker of my living actions,
To keep mine honour from corruption,
But such an honest chronicler as Griffith.
Whom I most hated living, thou hast made me,
With thy religious truth and modesty,[5]

[1] *Sought him*] Courted him.
[2] *Unsatisfied*] Never satisfied; insatiable.
[3] *You*] This pronoun addresses Ipswich and Oxford.
[4] *Happiness*] Good fortune.
[5] *Modesty*] Moderation; fairness.

Now in his ashes honour: Peace be with him!
Patience, be near me still; and set me lower.
I have not long to trouble thee.—Good Griffith,
Cause the musicians play me that sad note
I named my knell, whilst I sit meditating
On that celestial harmony I go to.

Sad and solemn music.

Grif. She is asleep: Good wench, let's sit down quiet,
For fear we wake her;—Softly, gentle Patience.

*The Vision. Enter, solemnly tripping one after another, six
Personages, clad in white robes, wearing on their heads
garlands of bays, and golden vizards on their faces;
branches of bays, or palm, in their hands. They first con-
gee to her, then dance; and at certain changes, the first
two hold a spare garland over her head; at which, the
other four make reverent curtsies; then the two that held
the garland deliver the same to the other next two, who
observe the same order in their changes, and holding the
garland over her head; which done, they deliver the same
garland to the last two, who likewise observe the same
order; at which, (as it were by inspiration,) she makes
in her sleep signs of rejoicing, and holdeth up her hands
to heaven: and so in their dancing vanish, carrying the
garland with them. The music continues.*

Kath. Spirits of peace, where are ye? Are ye all
            gone?
And leave me here in wretchedness behind ye?
Grif. Madam, we are here.
Kath.   It is not you I call for:
Saw ye none enter, since I slept?
Grif.   None, madam.
Kath. No? Saw you not, even now, a blessed troop

Invite me to a banquet? whose bright faces
Cast thousand beams upon me, like the sun:
They promised me eternal happiness;
And brought me garlands, Griffith, which I feel
I am not worthy yet to wear: I shall,
Assuredly.

    Grif. I am most joyful, madam, such good dreams
Possess your fancy.

    Kath.   Bid the music leave.
They are harsh and heavy to me.   [*Music ceases.*

    Pat.   Do you note,
How much her grace is altered on the sudden?
How long her face is drawn. How pale she looks,
And of an earthy cold. Mark her eyes!

    Grif. She is going, wench; pray, pray.

    Pat.   Heaven comfort her!

Enter a Messenger.

    Mess. An't like your grace,—

    Kath.   You are a saucy fellow;
Deserve we no more reverence?

    Grif.   You are to blame,
Knowing she will not lose her wonted greatness,
To use so rude behaviour: go to, kneel.

    Mess. I humbly do entreat your highness' pardon:
My haste made me unmannerly: There is staying
A gentleman, sent from the king, to see you.

    Kath. Admit him entrance, Griffith: But this fellow
Let me ne'er see again.

             [*Exeunt* GRIFFITH *and* Messenger.

Re-enter GRIFFITH, *with* CAPUCIUS.

               If my sight fail not,
You should be lord ambassador from the emperor,
My royal nephew, and your name Capucius.

Cap. Madam, the same, your servant.

Kath.   O my lord,
The times and titles now are altered strangely
With me, since first you knew me.   But, I pray you,
What is your pleasure with me ?

Cap.   Noble lady,
First, mine own service to your grace ; the next,
The king's request that I would visit you ;
Who grieves much for your weakness, and by me
Sends you his princely commendations,
And heartily entreats you take good comfort.

Kath. O my good lord, that comfort comes too late ;
'T is like a pardon after execution :
That gentle physic, given in time, had cured me ;
But now I am past all comforts here, but prayers.
How does his highness ?

Cap.   Madam, in good health.

Kath. So may he ever do ! and ever flourish,
When I shall dwell with worms, and my poor name
Banished the kingdom !   Patience, is that letter
I caused you write, yet sent away ?

Pat.   No, madam.   [*Giving it to* KATH.

Kath. Sir, I most humbly pray you to deliver
This to my lord the king.

Cap.   Most willing, madam.

Kath. In which I have commended to his goodness
The model of our chaste loves, his young daughter :—
The dews of heaven fall thick in blessings on her !—
Beseeching him to give her virtuous breeding ;
(She is young, and of a noble modest nature ;
I hope she will deserve well ;) and a little
To love her for her mother's sake, that loved him,
Heaven knows how dearly.   My next poor petition
Is, that his noble grace would have some pity

Upon my wretched women, that so long
Have followed both my fortunes faithfully :
Of which there is not one, I dare avow,.
(And now I should not lie,[1]) but will deserve,
For virtue, and true beauty of the soul,
For honesty, and decent carriage,
A right good husband, let him be a noble ;
And, sure, those men are happy that shall have them.
The last is, for my men ;—they are the poorest,
But poverty could never draw them from me ;—
That they may have their wages duly paid them,
And something over to remember me by ;
If heaven had pleased to have given me longer life,
And able means, we had not parted thus.
These are the whole contents :—And, good my lord,
By that you love the dearest in the world,
As you wish christian peace to souls departed,
Stand these poor people's friend, and urge the king
To do me this last right.
   Cap.   By heaven, I will ;
Or let me lose the fashion of a man !
   Kath. I thank you, honest lord.   Remember me
In all humility unto his highness :
Say, his long trouble now is passing
Out of this world : tell him, in death I blessed him,
For so I will.—Mine eyes grow dim.—Farewell,
My lord.—Griffith, farewell.—Nay, Patience,
You must not leave me yet.   I must to bed ;
Call in more women.—When I am dead, good wench
Let me be used with honour ; strew me over

---

[1] *Now I should not lie*] Now, when I am a dying woman, I ought
surely to speak truth. Compare *K. Richard II.* ii. 1, ' For they
breathe truth that breathe their words in pain.'

With maiden flowers,[1] that all the world may know
I was a chaste wife to my grave: embalm me,
Then lay me forth: although unqueened, yet like
A queen, and daughter to a king, inter me.
I can no more.   [*Exeunt, leading* KATH.

---

[1] *Maiden flowers*] It was customary to strew flowers on the
grave at maiden burials. Hence the 'virgin crants and maiden
strewments' at Ophelia's burial, *Hamlet*, v. 1.

ACT V.

SCENE I.—*A Gallery in the Palace.*

Enter GARDINER, *Bishop of* Winchester, *a Page with a torch before him, met by* SIR THOMAS LOVELL.

Gar. It 's one o'clock, boy, is 't not?
Boy.   It hath struck.
Gar. These should be hours for necessities,
Not for delights;[1] times to repair our nature
With comforting repose, and not for us
To waste these times.—Good hour of night, Sir Thomas!
Whither so late?
    Lov.   Came you from the king, my lord?
    Gar. I did, sir Thomas; and left him at primero[2]
With the duke of Suffolk.
    Lov.   I must to him too,
Before he go to bed. I 'll take my leave.
    Gar. Not yet, sir Thomas Lovell. What 's the matter?
It seems you are in haste; an if there be
No great offence belongs to 't, give your friend
Some touch of your late business:[3] Affairs that walk

---

[1] *Not for delights*] Gardiner refers to the king playing at cards with the duke of Suffolk.

[2] *Primero*] Supposed to be the most ancient game of cards in England; it was very fashionable in Shakspeare's time.

[3] *Some touch, &c.*] Some knowledge of your business at this late hour.

(As they say spirits do) at midnight, have
In them a wilder nature, than the business
That seeks despatch by day.

    Lov.   My lord, I love you;
And durst commend a secret to your ear
Much weightier than this work. The queen 's in labour,
They say, in great extremity; and feared,
She 'll with the labour end.

    Gar.   The fruit she goes with
I pray for heartily; that it may find .
Good time, and live : but for the stock, sir Thomas,
I wish it grubbed up now.

    Lov.   .   Methinks, I could
Cry the amen; and yet my conscience says
She 's a good creature, and, sweet lady, does
Deserve our better wishes.

    Gar.   But, sir, sir,—
Hear me, sir Thomas : You are a gentleman
Of mine own way; I know you wise, religious;
And, let me tell you, it will ne'er be well,—
T will not, sir Thomas Lovell, take 't of me,—
Till Cranmer, Cromwell, her two hands, and she,
Sleep in their graves.

    Lov.   Now, sir, you speak of two
The most remarked i' the kingdom. As for Cromwell —
Beside that of the jewel-house, he 's made master
O' the rolls, and the king's secretary; further, sir,
Stands in the gap and trade[1] of more preferments,
With which the time will load him : The archbishop
Is the king's hand and tongue : And who dare speak
One syllable against him ?

    Gar.   Yes, yes, sir Thomas,
There are that dare; and I myself have ventured

                [1] *Trade*] Road.

To speak my mind of him : and, indeed, this day,
Sir, (I may tell it you), I think I have
Incensed the lords o' the council, that he is
(For so I know he is, they know he is)
A most arch heretic, a pestilence
That does infect the land : with which they moved,
Have broken with the king ;[1] who hath so far
Given ear to our complaint, (of his great grace
And princely care, foreseeing those fell mischiefs
Our reason laid before him,) he hath commanded,
To-morrow morning to the council-board
He be convented. He 's a rank weed, sir Thomas,
And we must root him out. From your affairs
I hinder you too long : good night, sir Thomas.

    Lov. Many good nights, my lord ; I rest your servant.
                              [*Exeunt* GARDINER *and* Page.

  As LOVELL *is going out, enter the* KING, *and the* DUKE OF
               SUFFOLK.

    K. Hen. Charles, I will play no more to-night ;
My mind 's not on 't, you are too hard for me.
    Suf. Sir, I did never win of you before.
    K. Hen. But little, Charles ;
Nor shall not, when my fancy 's on my play.—
Now, Lovell, from the queen what is the news ?
    Lov. I could not personally deliver to her
What you commanded me, but by her woman
I sent your message ; who returned her thanks
In the greatest humbleness, and desired your highness
Most heartily to pray for her.
    K. Hen.   What say'st thou ? ha !
To pray for her ? what, is she crying out ?

---

   [1] *Have broken with the king*] Have broached the matter to the
king.

Lov. So said her woman; and that her sufferance made
Almost each pang a death.

    K. Hen.   Alas, good lady !

    Suf. God safely quit her of her burden, and
With gentle travail, to the gladdening of
Your highness with an heir !

    K. Hen.   'T is midnight, Charles,
Prithee to bed; and in thy prayers remember
The estate of my poor queen.   Leave me alone;
For I must think of that which company
Will not be friendly to.

    Suf.   I wish your highness
A quiet night, and my good mistress will
Remember in my prayers.

    K. Hen.   Charles, good night.

                               [*Exit* SUFFOLK.

          Enter SIR ANTHONY DENNY.

Well, sir, what follows ?

    Den. Sir, I have brought my lord the archbishop,
As you commanded me.

    K. Hen.   Ha ! Canterbury ?

    Den. Ay, my good lord.

    K. Hen.   'T is true : where is he, Denny ?

    Den. He attends your highness' pleasure.

    K. Hen.   Bring him to us.

                               [*Exit* DENNY.

    Lov. This is about that which the bishop spake ;
I am happily come hither.   [*Aside.*

      Re-enter DENNY, *with* CRANMER.

    K. Hen.   Avoid[1] the gallery.

                     [LOVELL *seems to stay.*

           [1] *Avoid*] Leave.

Ha!—I have said.—Be gone.

What?—   [*Exeunt* LOVELL *and* DENNY.

   Cran. I am fearful:—Wherefore frowns he thus?

'T is his aspect of terror.   All 's not well.

   K. Hen. How now, my lord?   You do desire to know

Wherefore I sent for you.

   Cran.   It is my duty

To attend your highness' pleasure.

   K. Hen.   .   Pray you, arise,

My good and gracious lord of Canterbury.

Come, you and I must walk a turn together;

I have news to tell you; Come, come, give me your hand.

Ah, my good lord, I grieve at what I speak,

And am right sorry to repeat what follows:

I have, and most unwillingly, of late

Heard many grievous, I do say, my lord,

Grievous complaints of you; which, being considered,

Have moved us and our council, that you shall

This morning come before us; where, I know,

You cannot with such freedom purge yourself,

But that, till further trial in those charges

Which will require your answer, you must take

Your patience to you, and be well contented

To make your house our Tower: You a brother of us,[1]

It fits we thus proceed, or else no witness

Would come against you.

   Cran.   I humbly thank your highness;

And am right glad to catch this good occasion

Most thoroughly to be winnowed, where my chaff

And corn shall fly asunder: for, I know

There 's none stands under more calumnious tongues

Than I myself, poor man.

---

    [1] *A brother of us*]   One of our Council.

K. Hen   Stand up, good Canterbury;
Thy truth, and thy integrity, is rooted
In us, thy friend: Give me thy hand, stand up;
Prithee, let 's walk. Now, by my holy-dame,
What manner of man are you?   My lord, I looked
You would have given me your petition, that
I should have ta'en some pains to bring together
Yourself and your accusers, and to have heard you
Without indurance [1] further.
    Cran.   Most dread liege,
The good I stand on is my truth and honesty;
If they shall fail, I, with mine enemies,
Will triumph o'er my person; which I weigh not,
Being of those virtues vacant. I fear nothing [2]
What can be said against me.
    K. Hen.   Know you not
How your state stands i' the world, with the whole world?
Your enemies are many, and not small; their practices [3]
Must bear the same proportion; and not ever
The justice and the truth o' the question carries
The due o' the verdict with it. At what ease
Might corrupt minds procure knaves as corrupt
To swear against you! such things have been done.
You are potently opposed; and with a malice
Of as great size. Ween you of better luck,
I mean, in perjured witness, [4] than your Master,
Whose minister you are, whiles here he lived
Upon this naughty earth? Go to, go to;
You take a precipice for no leap of danger,
And woo your own destruction.

    [1] *Indurance*] Imprisonment.
    [2] *Nothing*] Not at all.
    [3] *Practices*] Schemes; devices.
    [4] *In perjured witness*] See Matt. xxvi. 60.

Cran.   God, and your majesty,
Protect mine innocence, or I fall into
The trap is laid for me!
   K. Hen.   Be of good cheer,
They shall no more prevail, than we give way to.
Keep comfort to you; and this morning see
You do appear before them; if they shall chance,
In charging you with matters, to commit you,
The best persuasions to the contrary
Fail not to use, and with what vehemency
The occasion shall instruct you: if entreaties
Will render you no remedy, this ring
Deliver them, and your appeal to us
There make before them.—Look, the good man weeps!
He 's honest, on mine honour. God's blest mother!
I swear he is true-hearted; and a soul
None better in my kingdom.—Get you gone,
And do as I have bid you.—[*Exit* CRANMER.] He has
        strangled
His language in his tears.

Enter an old Lady.

   Gent. [*Within.*] Come back. What mean you?
   Lady. I 'll not come back; the tidings that I bring
Will make my boldness manners.—Now, good angels
Fly o'er thy royal head, and shade thy person
Under their blessed wings!
   K. Hen.   Now, by thy looks
I guess thy message. Is the queen delivered?
Say, ay; and of a boy.
   Lady.   Ay, ay, my liege;
And of a lovely boy: The God of heaven
Both now and ever bless her—'t is a girl
Promises boys hereafter. Sir, your queen

Desires your visitation, and to be
Acquainted with this stranger ; 't is as like you
As cherry is to cherry.
    K. Hen.   Lovell,—

             Enter LOVELL.

  Lov.   Sir.
    K. Hen. Give her an hundred marks. I 'll to the queen.
                                 [*Exit* KING.
    Lady. An hundred marks ! By this light, I 'll have
       more.
An ordinary groom is for such payment.
I will have more, or scold it out of him.
Said I for this the girl is like to him ?
I will have more, or else unsay 't ; and now
While it is hot, I 'll put it to the issue.   [*Exeunt.*

SCENE II.—*Lobby before the Council-Chamber.*

Enter CRANMER ; Servants, Door-Keeper, *&c.,* attending.

    Cran. I hope I am not too late ; and yet the gentleman,
That was sent to me from the council, prayed me
To make great haste.   All fast ? what means this ?—
     Hoa ?
Who waits there ?—Sure, you know me ?
    D. Keep.   Yes, my lord ;
But yet I cannot help you.
    Cran.   Why ?
    D. Keep. Your grace must wait till you be called for.

           Enter Doctor BUTTS.

  Cran.   So.

Butts. This is a piece of malice. I am glad,
I came this way so happily : The king
Shall understand it presently.   [*Exit* Butts.
     Cran. [*Aside.*]   'T is Butts,
The king's physician ; as he passed along,
How earnestly he cast his eyes upon me !
Pray heaven, he sound not my disgrace ! [1]   For certain,
This is of purpose laid by some that hate me,
(God turn their hearts !   I never sought their malice,)
To quench mine honour : they would shame to make me
Wait else at door ; a fellow-counsellor,
Among boys, grooms, and lackeys.   But their pleasures
Must be fulfilled, and I attend with patience.

     Enter, at a window above, the King *and* Butts.

     Butts. I 'll show your grace the strangest sight,—
     K. Hen.   What 's that, Butts?
     Butts. I think your highness saw this many a day.
     K. Hen. Body o' me, where is it ?
     Butts.   There, my lord :
The high promotion of [2] his grace of Canterbury ;
Who holds his state at door, 'mongst pursuivants,
Pages, and footboys.
     K. Hen.   Ha ! 'T is he, indeed :
Is this the honour they do one another ?
'T is well there 's one above them yet.   I had thought
They had parted [3] so much honesty among them,
(At least, good manners,) as not thus to suffer
A man of his place, and so near our favour,
To dance attendance on their lordships' pleasures,
And at the door too, like a post with packets.

---

[1] *He sound not*]   He do not make known or publish.
[2] *The high promotion of*]   The high respect shown to.
[3] *Parted*]   Shared or possessed amongst them all.

By holy Mary, Butts, there 's knavery :
Let them alone, and draw the curtain close ;
We shall hear more anon.   [*Exeunt.*

The Council-Chamber.

Enter the Lord Chancellor, *the* DUKE OF SUFFOLK, EARL
OF SURREY, Lord Chamberlain, GARDINER, *and* CROMWELL.
The Chancellor *places himself at the upper end of the
table on the left hand ; a seat being left void above him,
as for the* ARCHBISHOP OF CANTERBURY. *The rest seat
themselves in order on each side.* CROMWELL *at the lower
end, as secretary.*

Chan. Speak to the business, master secretary ;
Why are we met in council ?
    Crom.   Please your honours,
The chief cause concerns his grace of Canterbury.
    Gar. Has he had knowledge of it ?
    Crom.   Yes.
    Gar.   Who waits there ?
    D. Keep. Without, my noble lords ?
    Gar.   Yes.
    D. Keep.   My lord archbishop ;
And has done half an hour, to know your pleasures.
    Chan. Let him come in.
    D. Keep.   Your grace may enter now.
            [CRANMER *approaches the council-table.*
    Chan. My good lord archbishop, I am very sorry
To sit here at this present, and behold
That chair stand empty : But we all are men,
In our own natures frail, and capable
Of our flesh ; [1] few are angels : out of which frailty,

---

[1] *Capable of our flesh*] Influenced by our carnal will or tendency.

And want of wisdom, you, that best should teach us,
Have misdemeaned yourself, and not a little,
Toward the king first, then his laws, in filling
The whole realm, by your teaching and your chaplains,
(For so we are informed,) with new opinions,
Divers and dangerous; which are heresies,
And, not reformed, may prove pernicious.

Gar. Which reformation must be sudden too,
My noble lords: for those that tame wild horses
Pace them not in their hands[1] to make them gentle;
But stop their mouths with stubborn bits, and spur them,
Till they obey the manage. If we suffer
(Out of our easiness, and childish pity
To one man's honour) this contagious sickness,
Farewell, all physic; and what follows then?
Commotions, uproars, with a general taint
Of the whole state: as, of late days, our neighbours,
The upper Germany,[2] can dearly witness,
Yet freshly pitied in our memories.

Cran. My good lords, hitherto, in all the progress
Both of my life and office, I have laboured,
And with no little study, that my teaching,
And the strong course of my authority,
Might go one way, and safely; and the end
Was ever to do well: nor is there living
(I speak it with a single heart, my lords,)
A man that more detests, more stirs against,
Both in his private conscience and his place,
Defacers of a public peace than I do.
Pray heaven the king may never find a heart

---

[1] *Pace them not, &c.*] Do not lead them about.
[2] *The upper Germany*] Alluding to the immoderate zeal of some of Luther's followers, which was the occasion of violent commotions in Saxony.

With less allegiance in it ! Men that make
Envy and crooked malice, nourishment,
Dare bite the best.[1] I do beseech your lordships,
That, in this case of justice, my accusers,
Be what they will, may stand forth face to face,
And freely urge against me.

    Suf.   Nay, my lord,
That cannot be; you are a counsellor,
And by that virtue,[2] no man dare accuse you.

    Gar. My lord, because we have business of more
         moment,
We will be short with you. 'T is his highness' pleasure,
And our consent, for better trial of you,
From hence you be committed to the Tower,
Where, being but a private man again,
You shall know many dare accuse you boldly,
More than, I fear, you are provided for.

    Cran. Ah, my good lord of Winchester, I thank you,
You are always my good friend; if your will pass,
I shall both find your lordship judge and juror,
You are so merciful : I see your end,
'T is my undoing : Love and meekness, lord,
Become a churchman better than ambition ;

---

   [1] *Dare bite the best*] Are bold enough to slander the most up-right.

   [2] *By that virtue*] By virtue of your rank. A peer had to lose his nobility by attainder, before his trial could be instituted. 'The honour of peers,' says Blackstone, 'is so highly tendered by the law, that it is much more penal to spread false reports of them, and certain other great officers of the realm, than of other men : scandal against them being called by the peculiar name of *scandalum magnatum* (scandal of nobles or magnates), and subjected to peculiar punishments by divers ancient statutes.' Compare what Gardiner, in the next speech, says of Cranmer being 'a private man again.'

Win straying souls with modesty [1] again.
Cast none away.   That I shall clear myself,
Lay all the weight ye can upon my patience,
I make as little doubt, as you do conscience
In doing daily wrongs.   I could say more,
But reverence to your calling makes me modest.

Gar. My lord, my lord, you are a sectary,
That 's the plain truth; your painted gloss discovers,
To men that understand you, words and weakness.

Crom. My lord of Winchester, you are a little,
By your good favour, too sharp; men so noble,
However faulty, yet should find respect
For what they have been: 't is a cruelty
To load a falling man.

Gar.   Good master secretary,
I cry your honour mercy; [2] you may worst
Of all this table say so.

Crom.   Why, my lord?

Gar. Do not I know you for a favourer
Of this new sect? ye are not sound.

Crom.   Not sound?

Gar. Not sound, I say.

Crom.   Would you were half so honest!
Men's prayers then would seek you, not their fears.

Gar. I shall remember this bold language.

Crom.   Do.
Remember your bold life too.

Chan.   This is too much.
Forbear, for shame, my lords.

Gar.   I have done.

---

[1] *Modesty*]   Moderation; gentleness.
[2] *I cry your honour mercy*]   I beg pardon of your honour.   So, in
As you Like it, iii. 5, 'Cry the man mercy.'

Crom.   And I.

Chan. Then thus for you, my lord,—It stands agreed,
I take it, by all voices, that forthwith
You be conveyed to the Tower a prisoner;
There to remain, till the king's further pleasure
Be known unto us. Are you all agreed, lords?

All. We are.

Cran.   I₃ there no other way of mercy,
But I must needs to the Tower, my lords?

Gar.   What other
Would you expect? You are strangely troublesome:
Let some o' the guard be ready there.

Enter Guard.

Cran.   For me?
Must I go like a traitor thither?

Gar.   Receive him,
And see him safe i' the Tower.

Cran.   Stay, good my lords;
I have a little yet to say. Look there, my lords;
By virtue of that ring, I take my cause
Out of the gripes of cruel men, and give it
To a most noble judge, the king, my master.

Cham. This is the king's ring.

Sur.   'T is no counterfeit.

Suf. 'Tis the right ring, by heaven: I told ye all,
When we first put this dangerous stone a rolling,
'Twould fall upon ourselves.

Nor.   Do you think, my lords,
The king will suffer but the little finger
Of this man to be vexed?

Cham.   'T is now too certain:
How much more is his life in value with him!
Would I were fairly out on't!

Crom.   My mind gave me,

In seeking tales and informations
Against this man, (whose honesty the devil
And his disciples only envy at,)
Ye blew the fire that burns ye: Now have at ye.

Enter KING, *frowning on them; takes his seat.*

   Gar. Dread sovereign, how much are we bound to
     heaven
In daily thanks, that gave us such a prince;
Not only good and wise, but most religious:
One that, in all obedience, makes the church
The chief aim of his honour; and, to strengthen
That holy duty, out of dear respect,
His royal self in judgment comes to hear
The cause betwixt her and this great offender.
   K. Hen. You were ever good at sudden commendations,
Bishop of Winchester. But know, I come not
To hear such flattery now; and in my presence,
They are too thin and base [1] to hide offences.
To me you cannot reach; you play the spaniel,
And think with wagging of your tongue [2] to win me;
But, whatsoe'er thou tak'st me for, I am sure,
Thou hast a cruel nature, and a bloody.
Good man, [*to* CRANMER] sit down. Now let me see the
     proudest,
He that dares most, but wag his finger at thee:
By all that 's holy, he had better starve,
Than but once think his place becomes thee not.
   Sur. May it please your grace,—

---

[1] *Thin and base*] Flimsy and servile.
[2] *With wagging of your tongue*] As a fawning spaniel wags his
tail.

K. Hen.   No, sir, it does not please me.
I had thought, I had had men of some understanding
And wisdom, of my council; but I find none.
Was it discretion, lords, to let this man,
This good man, (few of you deserve that title,)
This honest man, wait like a lousy footboy
At chamber-door? and one as great as you are?
Why, what a shame was this! Did my commission
Bid ye so far forget yourselves? I gave ye
Power as he was a counsellor to try him,
Not as a groom: There's some of ye, I see,
More out of malice than integrity,
Would try him to the utmost, had ye mean;
Which ye shall never have, while I live.
    Chan.   Thus far,
My most dread sovereign, may it like your grace
To let my tongue excuse all. What was purposed
Concerning his imprisonment, was rather
(If there be faith in men) meant for his trial,
And fair purgation to the world, than malice;
I am sure, in me.
    K. Hen.   Well, well, my lords, respect him.
Take him, and use him well; he's worthy of it.
I will say thus much for him, if a prince
May be beholden to a subject, I
Am, for his love and service, so to him.
Make me no more ado, but all embrace him;
Be friends, for shame, my lords.—My lord of Canterbury,
I have a suit which you must not deny me;
That is, a fair young maid that yet wants baptism,
You must be godfather, and answer for her.
    Cran. The greatest monarch now alive may glory
In such an honour: How may I deserve it,
That am a poor and humble subject to you?

K. Hen. Come, come, my lord, you'd spare your
          spoons; [1] you shall have
Two noble partners with you: the old duchess of Norfolk,
And lady Marquis Dorset: Will these please you?
Once more, my lord of Winchester, I charge you,
Embrace, and love this man.

Gar.   With a true heart,
And brother-love, I do it.

Cran.   ·   And let heaven
Witness, how dear I hold this confirmation.

K. Hen. Good man, those joyful tears show thy true
          . heart.
The common voice, I see, is verified
Of thee, which says thus, ' Do my lord of Canterbury
A shrewd turn,[2] and he is your friend for ever.'—
Come, lords, we trifle time away; I long
To have this young one made a christian.
As I have made ye one, lords, one remain;
So I grow stronger, you more honour gain.   ·   [*Exeunt.*

SCENE III.—*The Palace Yard.*

Noise and tumult within.   Enter Porter *and his* Man.

Port. You 'll leave your noise anon, ye rascals: Do you
take the court for Paris-garden?[3] ye rude slaves, leave
your gaping.[4]

----

[1] *You'd spare, &c.*] It was an ancient custom at christenings, for
the sponsors to present silver spoons as a gift to the child. These
were often called *apostle spoons*, from the handles having been at
one time formed into figures of some of the twelve Apostles.

[2] *A shrewd turn*] An ill turn.

[3] *Paris-garden*] This celebrated bear-garden, at the Bankside,
Southwark, was so called from Robert de Paris, who had a residence
there in the time of Richard II.

[4] *Gaping*] Shouting; roaring.

[*Within.*] Good master porter, I belong to the larder.

Port. Belong to the gallows, and be hanged, you rogue :
Is this a place to roar in?—Fetch me a dozen crab-tree
staves, and strong ones; these are but switches to them.—
I 'll scratch your heads : You must be seeing christenings? Do you look for ale and cakes [1] here, you rude
rascals?

Man. Pray, sir, be patient; 't is as much impossible
(Unless we sweep them from the door with cannons)
To scatter them, as 't is to make them sleep
On May-day morning; which will never be :
We may as well push against Paul's [2] as stir them.

Port. How got they in, and be hanged?

Man. Alas, I know not; How gets the tide in?
As much as one sound cudgel of four foot
(You see the poor remainder) could distribute,
I made no spare, sir.

Port.   You did nothing, sir.

Man. I am not Samson, nor sir Guy, nor Colbrand, [3] to
mow them down before me : but, if I spared any that had
a head to hit, either young or old, he or she, let me never
hope to see a chine again.

[*Within.*] Do you hear, master porter?

Port. I shall be with you presently, good master puppy.
—Keep the door close, sirrah.

Man. What would you have me do?

---

[1] *Ale and cakes*] A distribution of cakes and ale was usual on
festive occasions.

[2] *Paul's*] St. Paul's Cathedral.

[3] *Sir Guy, nor Colbrand*] Sir Guy of Warwick, nor Colbrand the
Danish giant. The defeat of the latter hero by the former, at Win-
chester, is one of the leading features of the old romance of Sir Guy.
See Ellis's *Early Metrical Romances.*

Port. What should you do, but knock them down by the
dozens? Is this Moorfields [1] to muster in?

Man. There is a fellow somewhat near the door, he
should be a brazier [2] by his face, for, o' my conscience,
twenty of the dog-days now reign in 's nose; all that stand
about him are under the line, they need no other penance :
That fire-drake [3] did I hit three times on the head, and
three times was his nose discharged against me; he
stands there, like a mortar-piece, to blow us. There
was a haberdasher's wife of small wit near him, that
railed upon me till her pink porringer [4] fell off her head,
for kindling such a combustion in the state. I missed the
meteor once, and hit that woman, who cried out, *Clubs!* [5]
when I might see from far some forty truncheoneers draw
to her succour, which were the hope of the Strand, where
she was quartered. They fell on; I made good my place;
at length they came to the broomstaff with me; I defied
them still; when suddenly a file of boys behind them,
loose shot, [6] delivered such a shower of pebbles, that I was
fain to draw mine honour in, and let them win the work:
The devil was amongst them, I think, surely.

Port. These are the youths [7] that thunder at a play-
house, and fight for bitten apples; that no audience, but

[1] *Moorfields*] This was the favourite walk of ordinary citizens.

[2] *Brazier*] A charcoal pan.

[3] *Fire-drake*] This term, originally denoting a fiery dragon,
came also to signify an *ignis fatuus*, and an artificial fire-work.

[4] *Her pink porringer*] Her hole-pierced, porringer-shaped, head-
dress.

[5] *Cried out,* Clubs!] Called for peace-officers with their staves.

[6] *Loose shot*] Armed with loose shot, that is, stones or gravel.

[7] *The youths, &c.*] The *'prentices* were the terror of the actors.
They frequented either the twopenny gallery or the sixpenny pit;
the latter place being a yard, unseated, in the middle of the theatre
and open to the sky.

the tribulation of Tower-hill, or the limbs of Limehouse,[1]
their dear brothers, are able to endure. I have some of
them *in Limbo Patrum*,[2] and there they are like to dance
these three days; besides the running banquet[3] of two
beadles, that is to come.

Enter the Lord Chamberlain.

Cham. Mercy o' me, what a multitude are here!
They grow still too, from all parts they are coming,
As if we kept a fair here! Where are these porters,
These lazy knaves?—Ye have made a fine hand, fellows.
There 's a trim rabble let in : Are all these
Your faithful friends o' the suburbs? We shall have
Great store of room, no doubt, left for the ladies,
When they pass back from the christening.
  Port.   An 't please your honour,
We are but men ; and what so many may do,
Not being torn a pieces, we have done :
An army cannot rule them.
  Cham.   As I live,
If the king blame me for 't, I 'll lay ye all
By the heels, and suddenly ; and on your heads
Clap round fines, for neglect: You are lazy knaves;
And here ye lie baiting of bumbards,[4] when
Ye should do service.—Hark, the trumpets sound ;
They are come already from the christening :

---

[1] *The tribulation, &c.*] The troublesome fellows of Tower-hill,
and their dear brothers, the limbs of Limehouse, were no doubt a
very rough portion of the populace, accustomed to brawls and noise.
[2] *In Limbo Patrum*] In custody. The *Limbus Patrum* was properly the place of ' the spirits in prison,' that is, of the fathers and
patriarchs awaiting the resurrection.
[3] *Running banquet*] The porter means a flogging.
[4] *Baiting of bumbards*] Refreshing yourselves at ale barrels.

Go, break among the press, and find a way out
To let the troop pass fairly ; or I 'll find
A marshalsea shall hold you play these two months.[1]
Port. Make way there for the princess.
Man. You great fellow, stand close up, or I 'll make
your head ache.
Port. You i' the camblet, get up o' the rail; I 'll pick
you o'er the pales else.   [*Exeunt.*

SCENE IV.—*The Palace.*[2]

Enter trumpets, sounding ; then Two Aldermen, Lord
Mayor, Garter, CRANMER, DUKE OF NORFOLK, *with his
marshal's staff,* DUKE OF SUFFOLK, *Two* Noblemen *bearing great standing bowls for the christening gifts ; then
Four* Noblemen *bearing a canopy, under which the*
DUCHESS OF NORFOLK, *godmother, bearing the child richly
habited in a mantle, &c.   Train borne by a* Lady : *then
follows the* MARCHIONESS OF DORSET, *the other godmother,
and* Ladies.   *The troop pass once about the stage, and*
Garter *speaks.*

Gart. Heaven, from thy endless goodness, send pros-
perous life, long, and ever happy, to the high and mighty
princess of England, Elizabeth.

        Flourish.   Enter KING *and Train.*

Cran. [*Kneeling.*] And to your royal grace, and the
        good queen,
My noble partners,[3] and myself, thus pray ;—

_____
[1] *A marshalsea shall hold, &c.*] A prison that shall keep you in
sport, &c.
[2] *The Palace*] This was the Palace at Greenwich.
[3] *Partners*] Fellow-sponsors.

All comfort, joy, in this most gracious lady,
Heaven ever laid up to make parents happy,
May hourly fall upon you!

K. Hen. Thank you, good lord archbishop;
What is her name?

Cran.   Elizabeth.

K. Hen   Stand up, lord.—
                        [*The* KING *kisses the child.*
With this kiss take my blessing: God protect thee!
Into whose hands I give thy life.

Cran.   Amen.

K. Hen. My noble gossips,[1] ye have been too prodigal:
I thank ye heartily; so shall this lady,
When she has so much English.

Cran.   Let me speak, sir
For heaven now bids me; and the words I utter
Let none think flattery, for they 'll find them truth.
This royal infant, (heaven still move about her!)
Though in her cradle, yet now promises
Upon this land a thousand thousand blessings,
Which time shall bring to ripeness: She shall be
(But few now living can behold that goodness)
A pattern to all princes living with her,[2]
And all that shall succeed: Saba [3] was never
More covetous of wisdom, and fair virtue,
Than this pure soul shall be: all princely graces,
That mould up such a mighty piece as this is,

---

[1] *Gossips*] The *gossips* or *gossibs*, were the sponsors at christenings, and were so called from the meaning of the component words, *God* and *sib*, the latter word signifying *akin*; the gossips contracted spiritual affinity with the child.

[2] *Living with her*] Contemporary.

[3] *Saba*] The queen of Sheba, who 'came from the uttermost parts of the earth to hear the wisdom of Solomon.'

With all the virtues that attend the good,
Shall still be doubled on her: truth shall nurse her,
Holy and heavenly thoughts still counsel her:
She shall be loved, and feared; [1] Her own shall bless her:
Her foes shake like a field of beaten corn,
And hang their heads with sorrow: Good grows with her:
In her days, every man shall eat in safety,
Under his own vine, what he plants, and sing
The merry songs of peace to all his neighbours.
God shall be truly known; and those about her
From her shall read the perfect ways of honour,
And by those claim their greatness, not by blood.
Nor shall this peace sleep with her: But as, when
The bird of wonder dies, the maiden phœnix,
Her ashes new create another heir,
As great in admiration [2] as herself,
So shall she leave her blessedness to one, [3]
(When heaven shall call her from this cloud of darkness,)
Who, from the sacred ashes of her honour,
Shall star-like rise, as great in fame as she was,
And so stand fixed: Peace, plenty, love, truth, terror,
That were the servants to this chosen infant,
Shall then be his, and like a vine grow to him; [4]
Wherever the bright sun of heaven shall shine,
His honour, and the greatness of his name,
Shall be, and make new nations: He shall flourish,
And, like a mountain cedar, reach his branches .

---

[1] *Feared*]   That is, by her enemies.

[2] *Admiration*]   Wonderfulness.

[3] *To one*]   Viz. to K. James.   Sylvester's Dedication of *Du Bartas* to K. James (1605) likens Elizabeth and James to the phœnix; and Knolles's Dedication of his *History of the Turks* to Elizabeth, calls her ' the rare Phœnix of her sex.'

[4] *Grow to him*]   Twine round him.

To all the plains about him :——Our children's children
Shall see this, and bless heaven.

 K. Hen.   Thou speakest wonders.

 Cran. She shall be, to the happiness of England,
An aged princess ; many days shall see her,
And yet no day without a deed to crown it.
Would I had known no more ! but she must die,
She must, the saints must have her ; yet a virgin,
A most unspotted lily, shall she pass
To the ground, and all the world shall mourn her.

 K. Hen. O lord archbishop,
Thou hast made me now a man ; never before
This happy child did I get anything.
This oracle of comfort [1] has so pleased me,
That, when I am in heaven, I shall desire
To see what this child does, and praise my Maker.
I thank ye all :—to you, my good lord mayor,
And you, good brethren, I am much beholding ;
I have received much honour by your presence,
And ye shall find me thankful. Lead the way, lords ;
Ye must all see the queen, and she must thank ye,
She will be sick else. [2] This day, no man think
He has business at his house ; for all shall stay ;
This little one shall make it holiday.   [*Exeunt.*

---

 [1] *This oracle of comfort*] The comforting passage you have
uttered.

 [2] *She will be sick else*] She will be ill indeed, if she cannot be
seen by you on this occasion.

LaVergne, TN USA
29 November 2010
206737LV00001B/132/P